Mental Health Counselor:
A Career Guide

Mental Health Counselor: A Career Guide

Alexis Hammond

Larsen & Keller
www.larsen-keller.com

Mental Health Counselor: A Career Guide
Alexis Hammond
ISBN: 979-8-88836-099-6 (Hardback)

Larsen & Keller
Published by Larsen and Keller Education,
5 Penn Plaza,
19th Floor,
New York, NY 10001, USA

Cataloging-in-Publication Data

Mental health counselor : a career guide / Alexis Hammond.
p. cm.
Includes bibliographical references and index.
ISBN 979-8-88836-099-6
1. Mental health counselors--Vocational guidance. 2. Mental health counseling--Vocational guidance.
3. Mental health services--Vocational guidance. I. Hammond, Alexis.
RC466 .M46 2023
362.204 256--dc23

For more information regarding Larsen and Keller Education and its products, please visit the publisher's website www.larsen-keller.com

Table of Contents

Preface

There has been a steep rise in depression, anxiety and stress in our world today owing to our modern lifestyles. This is due to our ever-rising involvement with technology use and social media outlets, lesser social interaction and increased isolation. This situation is further compounded by our conscious drive to achieve greater academic and professional success to stay relevant in a highly competitive world. Therefore, counseling and therapy becomes imperative to achieve psychological resilience, deal with life's challenges and create a mental health balance. A mental health counselor (MHC) is a person working with individuals, families, couples and groups for promoting optimum mental and emotional health. Such a professional may be trained in specific therapeutic techniques for managing issues such as anxiety, depression, suicidal impulses, grief, family, parenting and marital problems, substance abuse, addictions, self-esteem issues, etc. This book is a valuable compilation of topics, ranging from the basic to the most complex theories and practices in the field of mental health counseling. It also offers a step-by-step guide to a career in mental health counseling. Coherent flow of topics, student-friendly language and extensive use of examples make this book an invaluable source of knowledge.

A foreword of all Chapters of the book is provided below:

Chapter 1 - The psychological well-being of an individual or the absence of any mental illness is termed as mental health. It encompasses the perceived autonomy, self-efficacy, dependence, competence and the self-realization of emotional and intellectual potential. Some of the factors affecting mental health include anxiety, stress, depression, grief, etc. This chapter discusses the varied facets of mental health and mental health counseling; **Chapter 2 -** A mental health counselor is someone who works with individuals and groups for promoting emotional and mental well-being. Assisting individuals with issues such as substance abuse, addiction, relationship issues, stress management, aging, etc. are the responsibility of a mental health counselor. This chapter has been carefully written to provide a understanding of the career path of a mental health counselor or a mental health technician, and some of the basics of these professions; **Chapter 3 -** Mental disorders are defined as psychological conditions that are characterized by disorganization of the mind, personality and emotions to that extent so as to impair significantly the normal psychological and social functioning of an individual. The treatments of these conditions include psychotherapy and medications, such as anti-depressants and anti-psychotics. The diverse mental health treatments for treating depression during pregnancy, anxiety disorder, delusional disorder, bipolar disorder, postpartum psychosis, social anxiety, schizophrenia, etc. have been extensively discussed in this chapter; **Chapter 4 -** Certain practices and lifestyle choices can ensure mental health for all individuals. Activities such as sports, cycling and athletics, meditation, recreation and occupational therapies, walks, crafts making, music therapy, dance therapy, art therapy, etc. can promote healing and rejuvenation on a psychological level. This chapter closely examines the techniques of improving mental health by targeting specific aspects of memory, mental strength, mental stamina, brain age and nourishment, for a holistic understanding of mental health.

I would like to thank the entire editorial team who made sincere efforts for this book and my family who supported me in my efforts of working on this book. I take this opportunity to thank all those who have been a guiding force throughout my life.

Alexis Hammond

CHAPTER 1 Understanding Mental Health

The psychological well-being of an individual or the absence of any mental illness is termed as mental health. It encompasses the perceived autonomy, self-efficacy, dependence, competence and the self-realization of emotional and intellectual potential. Some of the factors affecting mental health include anxiety, stress, depression, grief, etc. This chapter discusses the varied facets of mental health and mental health counseling.

Mental health is a state of wellbeing in which the individual realises his or her own abilities, can cope with the normal stresses of life, can work productively and fruitfully and is able to make a contribution to his or her own community.

The definition of 'mental ill health' or 'mental health problems' covers a very wide spectrum, from the worries and grief we all experience as part of everyday life to the most bleak, suicidal depression or complete loss of touch with everyday reality.

There are many issues that impact on our mental health including our physical health, our social situation, our living environment and genetic factors. This makes us all at risk of developing a mental health problem at any time during our lives. The most important thing to realise about mental health problems is that the majority of people who experience them do recover or learn to manage their mental health problem and still lead meaningful and fulfilled lives.

What are Mental Health Problems

'Mental health problems', 'mental illness' and 'mental ill health' are all common terms that are used to refer to the full spectrum of diagnosed clinical conditions such as depression, anxiety, psychosis, bipolar or schizophrenia. Symptoms of mental health problems have traditionally been divided into groups called either 'neurotic' or 'psychotic' symptoms. 'Neurotic' covers those symptoms which can be regarded as extreme forms of 'normal' emotional experiences such as depression, anxiety or panic. Conditions formerly referred to as 'neuroses' are now more frequently called 'common mental health problems,' although this does not always mean they are less severe than conditions with psychotic symptoms.

Less common are 'psychotic' symptoms which interfere with a person's perception of reality and may include hallucinations, delusions or paranoia, with the person seeing, hearing, smelling, feeling or believing things that no one else does. Psychotic symptoms or 'psychoses' are often associated with 'severe mental health problems.'

However, there is no sharp distinction between the symptoms of common and severe mental health problems. It is important to remember that some illnesses feature both neurotic and psychotic symptoms.

Common Disorders

The most common types of mental illness are anxiety disorders, mood disorders, and schizophrenia disorders; below we explain each in turn:

Anxiety Disorders

Anxiety disorders are the most common types of mental illness.

The individual has a severe fear or anxiety, which is linked to certain objects or situations. Most people with an anxiety disorder will try to avoid exposure to whatever triggers their anxiety.

Examples of anxiety disorders include:

- Panic disorder - the person experiences sudden paralyzing terror or a sense of imminent disaster.
- Phobias - these may include simple phobias (a disproportionate fear of objects), social phobias (fear of being subject to the judgment of others), and agoraphobia (dread of situations where getting away or breaking free may be difficult). We really do not know how many phobias there are - there could be thousands of types.
- Obsessive-compulsive disorder (OCD) - the person has obsessions and compulsions. In other words, constant stressful thoughts (obsessions), and a powerful urge to perform repetitive acts, such as hand washing (compulsion).
- Post-traumatic stress disorder (PTSD) - this can occur after somebody has been through a traumatic event - something horrible or frightening that they experienced or witnessed. During this type of event, the person thinks that their life or other people's lives are in danger. They may feel afraid or feel that they have no control over what is happening.

Mood Disorders

These are also known as affective disorders or depressive disorders. Patients with these conditions have significant changes in mood, generally involving either mania (elation) or depression. Examples of mood disorders include:

- Major depression - the individual is no longer interested in and does not enjoy activities and events that they previously liked. There are extreme or prolonged periods of sadness.
- Bipolar disorder - previously known as manic-depressive illness, or manic depression. The individual switches from episodes of euphoria (mania) to depression (despair).
- Persistent depressive disorder - previously known as dysthymia, this is mild chronic (long term) depression. The patient has similar symptoms to major depression but to a lesser extent.
- SAD (seasonal affective disorder) - a type of major depression that is triggered by lack of daylight. It is most common in countries far from the equator during late autumn, winter, and early spring.

Schizophrenia Disorders

Whether or not schizophrenia is a single disorder or a group of related illnesses has yet to be fully determined. It is a highly complex condition. Schizophrenia normally begins between the ages of 15 and 25. The individual has thoughts that appear fragmented; they also find it hard to process information.

Schizophrenia has negative and positive symptoms. Positive symptoms include delusions, thought disorders, and hallucinations. Negative symptoms include withdrawal, lack of motivation, and a flat or inappropriate mood.

How to Know when to Get Mental Health Counseling

Whether you're reeling from a traumatic event or can't seem to get out of an emotional rut, seeking out mental health counseling can be a helpful way to get back on track. Since everyone experiences grief, sadness, and stress it can be hard to know when it's time to see a professional. By knowing what red flags to look for and how to go about getting help, you can start on the road to feeling better.

Method 1. Recognizing you Need Help

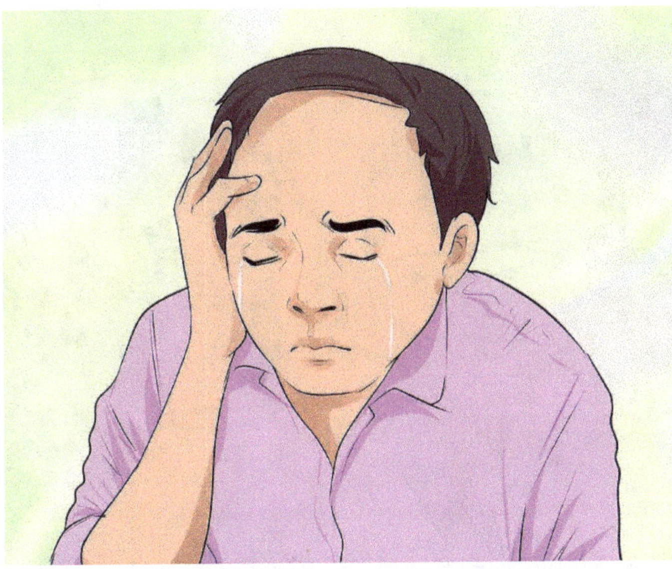

1. Deal with depression. Everyone gets down sometimes, but persistent feelings of hopelessness, despair, loss of interest or anxiety lasting more than two weeks can be indicative of clinical depression.

- If the symptoms become severe enough that they are disrupting daily activities or your quality of life, a counselor or health professional might be able to get you feeling more like your old self.

2. Recognize signs of bipolar disorder. Although no one knows what causes bipolar disorder, it seems to run in families and is a mood disorder that can severely affect your life.

- Bipolar disorder can be tricky to diagnose and its symptoms vary. But the main signs to look for are dramatic and unpredictable mood swings. A person with bipolar can have bouts of mania where they become excessively happy, a swell in energy and grand, racing thoughts. This mania is often followed by bouts of depression that can bring anxiety, sadness and even suicidal thoughts.

3. Know about schizophrenia. Contrary to public opinions on schizophrenia, it rarely comes with multiple personalities and is almost always a non-violent mental illness. If you're dealing with any of the symptoms of schizophrenia, see your doctor quickly to manage the illness.

- Schizophrenia is a serious disease and can cause difficulties in distinguishing between reality and the imaginary. This can mean you are seeing things that aren't there, paranoia, extreme fixations, and other bizarre behaviors that can rapidly erode one's ability to live a normal life.

4. Deal with anxiety. We all feel anxiety from time to time but for some people it can be a crippling experience. If you're having anxiety that affects your ability to function either at work or socially, you may have a generalized disorder.

- Anxiety can be marked by excessive worry regularly for at least six months, irritability, sleep problems and other general negative feelings.
- There are different types of anxiety that can be brought upon by certain situations or triggers. For example, if everyday social situations trigger anxiety you may have social anxiety disorder. Other types of anxiety include panic disorder, a feeling of sudden terror accompanied by physical symptoms or phobias that are triggered by events like flying or specific objects, like spiders.

5. Get help processing trauma. Many times, individuals have trouble coping with a recent trauma, such as a car accident, child abuse, sexual assault or loss of a loved one. Although grief and sadness are normal emotions, a mental health counselor can help make the process easier.

- If you are experiencing debilitating and persistent difficulties, seeking out help might make your coping easier. Some of these symptoms may include: anger, fear, anxiety, racing heartbeat and difficulty sleeping. It is normal to feel these after a trauma but if they are disrupting your life and months pass with no alleviation, you may need an expert to help.

6. Help your relationship. Sometimes it's not just an individual that needs help but partners in an unhealthy relationship. If your relationship with your significant other is increasingly a point of stress and contention, you might benefit from professional counseling.

- It's always difficult to recognize and admit problems in your relationship. If you notice you and your significant other having trouble communicating, arguing with increased regularity, and find one another a source of stress, it might be time to seek outside help. Every relationship has issues, but remaining vigilant about early problems could save you and your partner down the road.

Method 2. Looking for Signs

1. Watch for dramatic mood swings. Dramatic mood swings may be an indication that counseling is useful for your mental health or the presence of a mental illness. Beyond normal moodiness during puberty, pregnancy, menopause or other stressful life events, serious mood swings can be an indication of a larger problem.

- Mood swings are excessive or abrupt changes in your frame of mind or emotional status. For example, you may shift from euphoria to extreme sadness abruptly and often with no environmental trigger. These can indicative of mental health issues like bi-polar or a personality disorder. If you notice yourself or a friend experiencing persistent, worsening, mood swings, you should seek out mental health help.

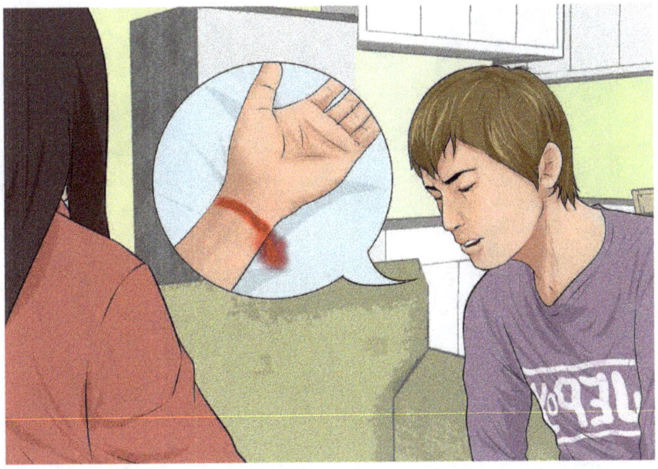

2. Seek help immediately if you have suicidal thoughts. If you or anyone you know is thinking about suicide, you should seek professional help immediately. Whether you're thinking about taking your own life, or suspect a friend, it's important to recognize this and seek help.

- Suicidal behavior and tendencies can vary from individual to individual. Some telltale signs include: talking about suicide, seeking out means of self-harm (such as pills or a gun), withdrawing from all social contact, rapid personality changes or engaging in risky, self-destructive behavior.
- There's help. Suicidal thoughts can be scary and even embarrassing but no one needs to face it alone. You should reach out to a close friend or loved one and make an appointment with a counselor. If these aren't options, call a suicide prevention hotline like 800-273-TALK.

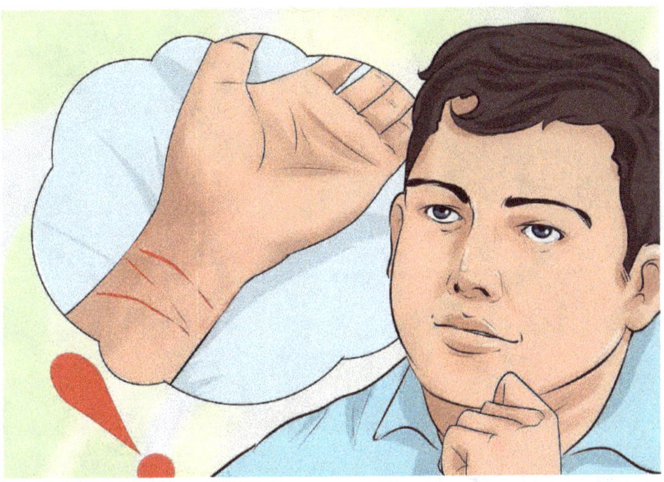

3. See if you're prone to self-harming. Although suicide is an extreme version of self-harm, other forms can be an indication of emotional pain and distress that could benefit from a professional.

- Self-harm can include cutting one's skin, burning one's self or even sticking objects in your skin. If you notice a friend who may be doing these, or if you are yourself, there are safer long-term ways to deal with stresses that cause self-harm.

4. Get help if you struggle with substance abuse. Addiction and mental health have strong links and individuals often self-medicate. If you or a friend increasingly find drugs or alcohol as a way to cope with emotional issues like stress or anger, it might be time to seek out help in order to find safer alternatives.

- Although it's fine for legal aged adults to have a drink to unwind, there are early warning signs that an over reliance on substances may be problematic. These include a family history of addiction, neglecting responsibilities because of substance use, dangerous and reckless behavior while intoxicated, needing more of a substance for the desired effect and spending increased time thinking and using the substance. If you notice these characteristics in yourself or someone you know, a mental health counselor may be able to find other more healthy coping mechanisms.

Method 3. Choosing to Get Counseling

1. Talk to your primary care physician. It can be overwhelming to navigate all of the options for mental health counseling. Your primary care physician will have experience dealing with medical conditions like depression and can recommend your next step.

- Let your doctor give you a mental health evaluation. Your doctor will be able to assess whether your struggles will benefit from counseling or whether medical treatment is necessary. Many mental illnesses like depression or bipolar disorder can be helped with medication.

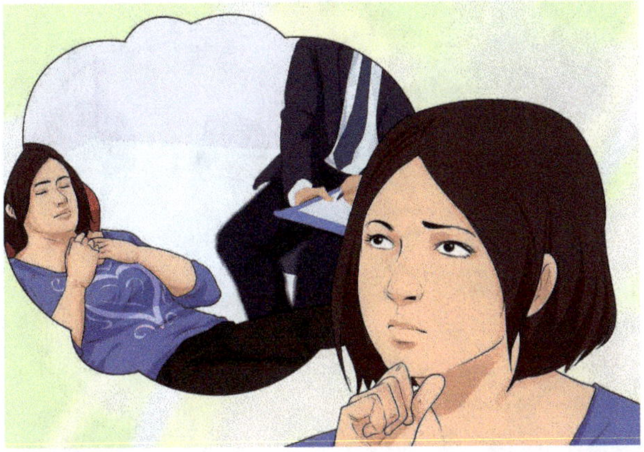

2. Determine what type of counseling you require. Using your doctor and other resources, you'll need to decide what sort of counselor to seek out. This can vary depending on for what you're seeking help.

- If you think talk-based therapy will help you, there are licensed therapists and social workers. These can range from those with master's degrees to doctorates in psychology. With the help of your doctor you may decide that a psychiatrist and biological approach using medicine will be most helpful. If your relationship needs help, licensed marriage or relationship counselors may be best.

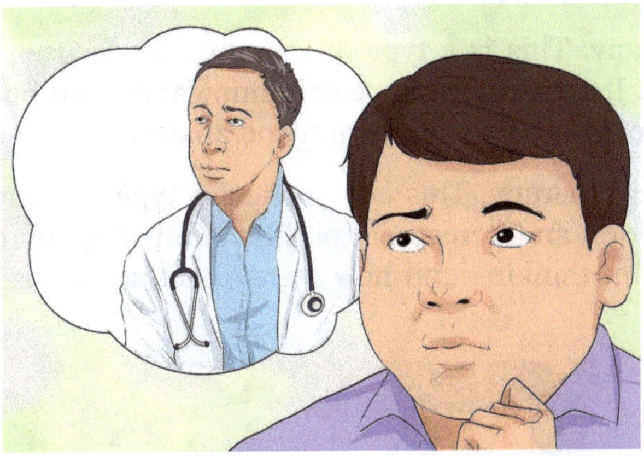

3. Locate a mental health professional. Once you know what type of counseling may work best for you, you'll have to start narrowing down concrete options.

- Use your doctor. Your doctor likely has experience dealing with mental health as well as knowledge of your medical history. They may be able to recommend a colleague they think will be a good fit.
- Look online. You have to be careful about this but a simple search can bring you options in your area as well as reviews. You can always contact the professional before meeting to assess whether they can help you and the experience they have in treating similar problems.
- Check with your health insurance provider. If you have insurance, this will not only help from a cost standpoint but they may also be able to help facilitate you finding the specific help you need.

4. Know what to expect. Once you decide it's time to get help, you'll have a lot of different options open to you. Based on your physician's advice, the nature of your problem, and your own research you can find the type of therapy that's best for you.

- Individual therapy. Individual psychotherapy usually entails sitting down one on one with a mental health professional, talking about your problems and taking steps to address your issues in a healthy way. This could be through talk therapy or more traditional methods like psychoanalysis that try to uncover subconscious issues.
- Group therapy. You may do better in a group setting where a support group is guided by the expertise of a mental health professional.
- Interpersonal therapy. This is a type of therapy that focuses on how you interact with friends and family. It seeks to improve communication and build up self-esteem and can address a number of issues like depression and anxiety.
- Cognitive behavioral therapy. This is a particular type of therapy that attempts identify and change behavioral and perceptual problems causing distress. This can be helpful in creating new ways of thinking and new ways of acting that reinforce positive emotional well being.

5. Be open and honest about your feelings. It can be really hard and even scary to admit that you're struggling. If you experience any of the above signs, seeking out help as soon as possible.

- Sometimes it can be hard to talk to a doctor or stranger about your deep feelings. If you have a trusted friend, family member or someone like a pastor, they may be a more comfortable place to start. It is always easier to share your burden with someone you trust and care about.

- Make sure you're comfortable with your therapist. It can be hard to discuss such personal, often painful feelings if you are not comfortable and trusting with your choice. If you find you don't click with your first choice, don't be afraid to explore other options. As you get further into the process you will start to gain a clearer understanding of what makes you comfortable and what works best for you.

CHAPTER

2 Becoming a Mental Health Counselor

A mental health counselor is someone who works with individuals and groups for promoting emotional and mental well-being. Assisting individuals with issues such as substance abuse, addiction, relationship issues, stress management, aging, etc. are the responsibility of a mental health counselor. This chapter has been carefully written to provide a understanding of the career path of a mental health counselor or a mental health technician, and some of the basics of these professions.

Mental Health Counselor

A mental health counselor is a professional who utilizes a variety of psychotherapy methods and techniques to help people experiencing psychological distress. The prevalence of mental health problems highlights the demand and need for qualified professionals to diagnose, treat, and prevent mental health issues.

All people face different psychological challenges at various points in life, and sometimes people need the help of a professional to cope with these difficulties. It can sometimes be confusing to determine what type of help is needed, particularly because there are so many different types of professionals who specialize in treating mental health issues.

Mental health counselors represent just one profession that specifically works with people dealing with cognitive, behavioral, and emotional issues. Counselors work with individuals, families, groups, and communities to deal with mental health issues and improve mental well-being.

You might find professional mental health counselors working in a wide range of settings including:

- Mental health clinics
- Schools
- Private practice
- Hospitals
- Community health centers
- Correctional facilities
- Businesses
- Colleges and universities
- Social service agencies
- Government agencies

People experiencing symptoms of psychological illnesses such as depression, phobias, and anxiety may choose to see a mental health counselor for counseling and psychotherapy services. Counselors may also help people experiencing social difficulties, emotional problems, addictions and substance abuse, grief, self-esteem issues, and marital difficulties. Some mental health counselors choose to work with specific populations such as children, the elderly, or college students.

Some of the tasks that a mental health counselor may tackle on a regular basis include:

- Assessing and diagnosing clients experiencing symptoms of psychological distress.
- Providing psychotherapy to clients.
- Talking to clients about their experiences, emotions, and thoughts.
- Conducting group sessions with families.
- Working with clients to set goals, develop a treatment plan, and gain insight through treatment.
- Working with clients to identify situations, behaviors, and thoughts that interfere with their wellness and recovery.
- Examining social issues that may influence a clients mental well-being including peer pressure, bullying, substance use, prejudice, work stress, financial challenges, and health issues.
- Referring clients to other health professionals as well as to other resources in the community such as other social services, job services, and support groups.

Counseling tends to view individual needs within a developmental context. Rather than focusing on dysfunction, counselors often see problems as arising from normal reactions to developmental changes or as difficulty dealing with specific life stages. As a result, counselors may focus on personal development by helping you learn the skills and coping abilities you need to deal with such life changes and stages effectively.

While counselors are often called upon to treat specific problems, they also tend to take an approach that focuses on overall wellness. Dealing with the immediate problem is important, but counselors also strive to help you function not just minimally, but optimally. Enhancing overall well-being by solving problems, improving resilience, encouraging healthy behaviors, and improving relationships are key components of counselors' duties.

How to Become a Mental Health Counselor

Step 1: Complete a bachelor's degree in a behavioral, social science, or psychology field.

Because a master's degree is a requirement for licensure as a mental health counselor, pursuing a bachelor's degree in counseling related fields sets the groundwork for graduate studies in counseling. Coursework for undergraduate studies in these fields will typically include the evaluation of human development, counseling skills and foundation, introduction to psychology, and basic approaches to counseling/therapy.

Step 2: Earn a master's degree in mental health counseling.

There are many CACREP accredited universities that offer studies specifically in mental health counseling. Obtaining your graduate degree in mental health counseling is a requirement for for practice as a licensed professional mental health counselor.

Step 3: Complete graduate and postgraduate internship experience for certification/licensure requirements.

As a crucial aspect of accredited counseling master's programs, graduate supervised counseling experience allows students to dive into their future role as a licensed professional mental health counselor, gaining hands-on experience under licensed professional counselors.

Step 4: Pass any required counseling exams for licensure.

Some states and counseling programs require the passing of a recognized counseling examination for gradation or licensure such as the National Counselor Examination (NCE) and the National Clinical Mental Health Counseling Examination (NCMHCE).

Step 5: Apply for and earn additional mental health certifications.

Licensed professional counselors can pursue a national certification through the National Board of Certified Counselors (NBCC). Mental health counselors can also pursue specializations in grief, pastoral, school-based mental health counseling, or other mental health challenges, concerns, or disorders.

Step 6: Continue your education and stay up to date on mental health counseling trends and changes.

Continuing education is imperative to maintaining professional counseling licensure and keeping in the know on changes, updates, and movements in trends on mental health care, counseling, and client advocacy.

How to Become a Licensed Mental Health Counselor

You've done some career exploration, and learned what mental health counselors do and how they help people. Now you're thinking about becoming a licensed mental health counselor. With the right education and a license, you can do just that.

Method 1. Getting your Education

1. Earn your bachelor's degree. The first step in becoming a licensed mental health counselor is to obtain your bachelor's degree. Most likely your degree would be a Bachelor of Arts (BA) or Bachelor of Science (BS) in psychology or a related field.

- Once accepted and in school, take opportunities to join student organizations and do research. These activities can give valuable experience and allow you to meet people for future networking and professional growth.
- As part of the four year BA or BS program of study, you'll need to take upper-division credit hours in social sciences (psychology and sociology). Research methods and statistics can be helpful too, and may be required.
- Do your best to keep your GPA up. Making good grades will make it much easier to get into graduate school.
- Look into internships that you can do during your BA program as well. This can help you to figure out what you might like to specialize in later on or if you actually want to pursue a career as a counselor. For example, you might intern at a women's shelter or for a crisis line.

2. Get your master's degree. Obtaining a Master of Arts (MA), Master of Science (MS) or equivalent degree is the next step in becoming a licensed mental health counselor. Some states require that the degree program is accredited by the Council for Accreditation of Counseling and Related

Educational Programs. Check with your state licensing board to determine what their requirements are.

- Take the Graduate Record Exam. This test measures your critical thinking skills and is required in order to be admitted into graduate school. Study for it well in advance, but don't worry if you have to take it more than once. Many people do.
- Many programs have a multi-part application process. It often includes submitting essays, undergraduate records, letters of recommendation, and an interview process. Begin the process early so you have enough time to complete the process and meet all deadlines.
- Make the most of opportunities to participate in research and in student and national organizations in the field of mental health counseling like the American Mental Health Counselors Association.

3. Think about earning your doctorate. Some licensed mental health counselors go on to earn their PhD in order to make themselves more marketable and to gain more experience and knowledge. However, this is optional. You need a Master's degree to be a licensed counselor, but you do not need a PhD.

- Use resources like the U.S. Department of Labor Bureau of Labor Statistics to determine if the additional years of school are worth the increase in income.

Method 2. Getting Licensed

1. Complete your practicum while you are in school. While you are completing your Master's

degree, you will need to complete a practicum. The practicum is an important part of getting a counseling degree. The practicum gives you supervised counseling experience and helps you to develop your counseling skills.

- You may be required to participate in a group practicum, individual practicum, and an externship. The externship may take place at a clinic or hospital while you are still in school, such as during the last two semesters of your program. A supervisor from your program will likely need to be on site for an externship as well.
- You usually need about 600 hours of practicum to meet your requirement.
- Keep in mind that practicum and externships are not something that you can just go out and get. They must be approved by your program director.

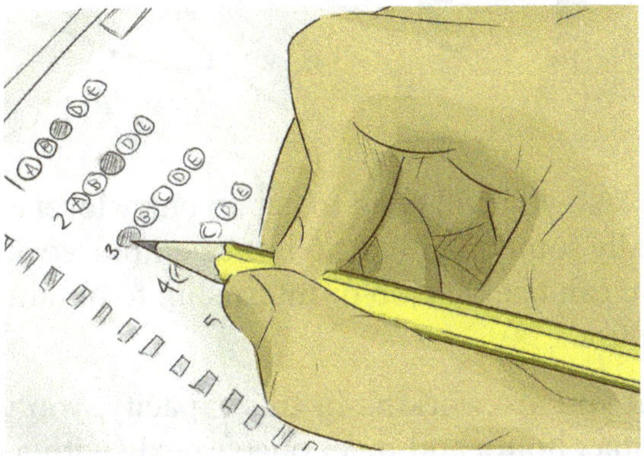

2. Take your NCE exam. After your practicum and your coursework is complete, you will need to sit for your NCE exam. You can usually do this towards the end of your last semester or after it is over. Some states also require an additional state exam, and all states have a jurisprudence exam. Find out about licensing requirements in your state to determine what tests you need to take.

- Check with the licensing board in your state to find out what tests you need to take, when the tests are offered, how much they cost, when you need to take them, and any other specific requirements you will need to know about.
- Prepare for the exam in advance by reviewing course material from your graduate program, participating in an exam preparation program, or joining a study group.

3. Send your passing NCE scores and proof of your practicum to the state board. After you pass

your NCE exam, you will need to send your passing scores and proof that you have completed your practicum (in-school clinical hours) to the state board to receive your provisional license.

- This license usually has a special term in it to indicate that it's provisional, such as "LPC-Intern" or "Licensed ASSOCIATE Counselor."

4. Find a job or internship. Next, you will need to get an entry level counseling job that requires a provisional license. It is usually something like an intake employee at a hospital, a case worker, or working for a non-profit. You can use this job or internship to obtain your required post-master's degree supervised clinical hours.

- During the years that you are working in this capacity, you will need to keep track of all your face-to-face contact hours and meet once weekly with a clinical supervisor to review your cases.

5. Submit proof of completion. Once you have completed all of the required hours at your job or internship, you will need to submit documentation to show that you have completed the required post-master's hours. You will need to submit this proof to the state board to receive a full license.

- You do not need to take any additional tests after this point.
- Full licensure is usually called something like "Licensed Professional Counselor" or "License Professional Clinical Counselor."

Method 3. Starting your Career

1. Determine your specialty. Because mental health counseling covers a range of areas (like

marriage and family counseling, psychotherapy, or substance abuse treatment) you will need to decide exactly which area or areas you want to specialize in.

- Some careers require additional training or experience in that area before you can begin practicing.
- Think about things like what setting you want to work in (a hospital, clinic, treatment center, etc.) and the types of clients you want to help.
- Take some time researching the area you are interested in to determine what the requirements are, how much you will make, and where you can practice (for example, private practice, in a counseling center, etc.)

2. Look into your job options. There are many different ways you can begin your counseling career. You may want to start your own independent practice, join an existing practice, work for a non-profit organization, or even a government agency. Think about the pros and cons of starting your career in each setting.

- Keep in mind that you will likely be paid during your post-licensing practicum or at least during your externship, even if it is just a stipend. During these experiences, you will also have a chance to experience different types of populations and figure out what population you want to work with.
- If benefits and security are important to you, you may want to join a practice or work for an agency.
- Consider joining an existing practice to gain experience and then opening your own practice.
- Research all of your options on sites the U.S. Department of Labor.
- Think about issues like liability and the opportunity to select your own clients rather than have them assigned to you.

3. Apply for a position. The final thing you need to do to become a licensed mental health counselor is to apply for a job (and get it) or open your own practice.

- Use the relationships and connections you made during graduate school and your residency to find out about job opportunities in your area.
- Search job boards and sites like LinkedIn to learn about mental health counseling positions that are available.
- When you get a job, then you can keep your position and get a pay bump after you are fully licensed, or you can leave to start your own practice. However, keep in mind that you cannot open a private practice in any state until you are fully licensed.
- Remember that you might not get the first position you apply for. Don't let it discourage you, just keep submitting your resume to agencies and centers and you will obtain a position.

How to Become a Mental Health Technician

The field for mental health professionals is growing rapidly due to mental health awareness. Many rewarding careers await those with the education, training, and desire to work as mental health professionals. Follow the steps below to become a mental health technician.

Method 1. Decide Which Mental Health Career is Right for you

Mental health technicians include a wide variety of mental health workers, but the term is perhaps most commonly used to refer to as medical assistants, nursing assistants, and physician assistants. In some cases, people use the term to describe psychologists, behavioral counselors, orderlies, and therapists. Deciding what type of career track appeals to you is an important part of becoming a mental health technician.

1. Determine how much education you are willing to get. Education programs and formal training can take nearly a decade for psychiatrists and medical doctors if you do not have a bachelors degree.

- Consider how much time (and money) you have available to get the necessary education and start working as a mental health technician.

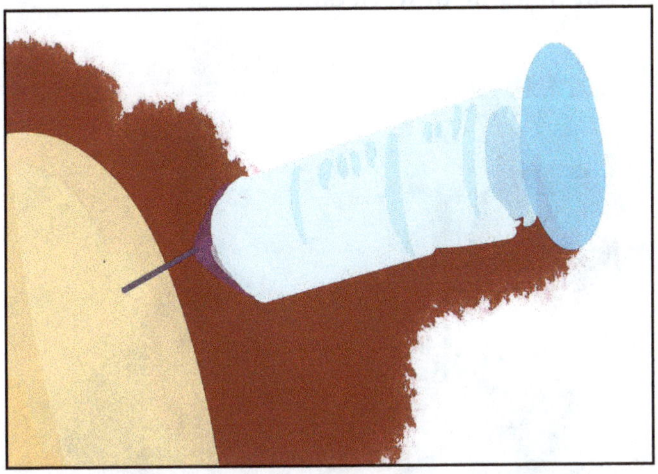

2. Evaluate your comfort level with the medical aspect of the field. Some mental health technicians regularly encounter blood and other bodily fluids on the job, and may interact with patients in a very medical manner.

- If you do not react well to medical situations, your mental health technician training may need to tend toward a position related to therapy, research, or administrative work.

Method 2. Enroll in a Formal Education or Training Program

Once you have decided what type of mental health technician you wish to become, look up specific job descriptions in that field and examine the requirements for education. If you need a specific degree, apply to a local school or online degree program and work on making yourself an appealing candidate to the admissions board and to future employers.

1. Make your application stand out with relevant experience. Programs that prepare students for work in the mental health field often want students who are passionate about the field and well aware of the type of career they are likely to have.

- If you are able, get some exposure to the type of job you wish to have by shadowing a professional in that field, volunteering at a crisis hotline, helping advocacy organizations, and getting a field for what that line of work entails.

2. Consider regular volunteer work or shadow experiences. Not only will repeated, long-term experience in this field help you gain admittance to a degree program, it will also prepare you for the type of work and interaction you will have with patients as a mental health technician.

- Regular, committed, relevant experience like this can often be maintained through the duration of a degree program, potentially leading to a job offer when your education is done. If not, it will at least serve as great experience to put on your resume when applying to jobs at the end of your program.

Method 3. Find a Mental Health Technician Job

Once you have the education or formal training, becoming a mental health technician can be just a job application away. Cast a wide net and be open to opportunities that are not exactly what you want, provided they keep you in the mental health field and leave you the chance to tailor your work or upgrade to your job of choice in the future.

1. Network to find opportunities in your field. If you have been volunteering or shadowing, ask whether that organization has any available positions. Even if they don't, they may be glad to put you in touch with friends, business partners, or colleagues with an opening who will be glad to have a personal referral.

- In addition, let friends, family members, neighbors, fellow students, and pretty much everyone you meet know that you are looking for work as a mental health technician.
- Use online professional networking sites like LinkedIn to post your resume and see whether people you know may be able to point you toward your next job.

2. Take advantage of online job search engines and print resources. Online job search engines, the newspaper, and even billboards at local mental health facilities can be excellent ways to find out what a wide variety of local companies have announced as job openings.

- Consider multiple ways to phrase the type of mental health technician position you are hoping to get, and scan anything you are even remotely qualified for to decide whether to apply.

- Set up automatic searches and email notifications with keywords like "mental health tech," "behavioral tech," "psychiatric," "counselor," or any other terms that will locate new jobs in your field – most websites can send them to you daily or weekly according to your preferences.

3. Cold call organizations to ask about job openings. Psychiatric wards, rehabilitation centers, local and state public health agencies, community clinics, charitable organizations, private psychiatric offices, alternative therapy clinics, and hospitals may all have relevant mental health technician positions.

- If you cannot find information about job openings on their website, consider calling and asking politely if they are hiring.
- You may wish to visit in person with a copy of your resume and a general cover letter explaining your wish to work as a mental health technician, describing your passion for the field and your most pertinent experience or education.

4. Promote yourself. Be vocal about your education, experience, and excitement for working as a mental health technician.

- Find ways to describe past work experience as relevant mental health technician experience; for instance, customer service experience can translate to comfort working with a wide variety of people (good for working with patients), bartending can be billed as experience listening to people's concerns and intimate problems, and being a college resident assistant can count as experience counseling homesick students and identifying alcohol abuse.

How to Get a Counseling License

A counseling license is generally a requirement for mental health counselors and school counselors who wish to practice in healthcare and educational settings. Licensing requirements vary by jurisdiction and job type. Though the general educational background and many state licensing guidelines are similar, professionals seeking licensure must still research local requirements in order to choose the best academic and professional path for their career goals.

Part 1. Getting the Right Education

1. Choose the type of counseling service. Counseling is actually a large umbrella of services, and most professionals choose a specific area of expertise in which to specialize. Examples of different counseling specializations include: academic counseling, mental health counseling, substance abuse counseling, domestic or child abuse counseling, career counseling, grief counseling, marriage counseling, etc.

2. Consider your work setting. Counselors work in substance abuse clinics, hospitals, private practices, social work facilities, schools, and universities. Deciding where you want to work can also help you determine the type of counseling you want to study.

3. Get an undergraduate degree in counseling or psychology. As an undergraduate counseling or psychology student, you can expect to study introductory courses, as well as courses heavy of statistical data and research methods. From there, you will additionally choose from upper-division courses that give you overviews of social, developmental, abnormal, and comparative psychology, which will help you in choosing a specific focus for graduate school if you haven't already decided on one. The better you do in your courses, the more options you're likely to have for graduate school.

- Your school may offer either a BA or a BS in psychology. Graduate schools do not weigh more heavily toward one or the other when reviewing applications.

4. Look for relevant extracurricular actives. Research projects, internships, and teaching assistant programs will all help you distinguish yourself when applying to graduate schools. Your department advisor can help you find available opportunities.

- Your campus may also have clubs related to psychology. Look into them and become an active member.
- Since psychology and counseling graduate programs are competitive, get as much experience under your belt as you can.

5. Take the GRE. Different institutions factor GRE scores into their applicant screening process in different ways. However, all graduate school applications for counseling programs will require that you take the GRE.

6. Apply to graduate programs. You will have to apply to psychology or counseling psychology graduate programs to earn either an MA or MS in counseling. Apply specifically to programs with a focus on the type of counseling you wish to perform as a professional. You should also apply to as many graduate schools as you can due to the highly competitive nature of the programs.

- MA programs often offer a more general approach to counseling whereas MS programs typically offer increased levels of specialization if you're already certain of the area in which you want to specialize.
- An advanced degree in social work is not the same as an advanced degree in counseling. Though the two professions have some instances of crossover, the boards that govern licensing for social workers are not the same as the boards that govern counseling licenses.
- Ensure that every program to which you apply is accredited by the Council for the Accreditation of Counseling and Related Educational Programs (CACREP), the Council on Rehabilitation Education (CORE), or one of the other accrediting bodies recognized by the licensing board in your state.

7. Study hard during graduate school. Counseling programs will provide substantial clinical or hands-on experience and coursework in human behavior and development, ethics, counseling strategies, etiology of mental illness, substance abuse disorders, and other areas. Doing well in your program is going to leave you more prepared for licensing requirements.

- You may also choose to go on to receive a doctoral degree in counseling. However, this isn't necessary to get a counseling license.

8. Apply for internship and residency programs. Once you finish school, most states require you to have a certain number of hours of experience counseling in a supervised, professional environment. Look into internships and residency programs to help you start accumulating the necessary hours of experience.

Part 2. Completing Licensing Requirements for your Jurisdiction

1. Search online for state websites that outline licensing requirements. Each locality has a different set of requirements and an application process that you must follow closely.

- You can find a link to each state's guidelines to become a Licensed Professional Counselor (LPC) here.
- Study the requirements. A New York State license for mental health counselors, for example, requires good moral character, a minimum age of 21, master's degree completion, a licensing exam, and 3,000 documented hours of post-graduate, supervised counseling experience. In addition, licensing applicants must have completed training that covers how to identify and report child abuse.

2. Speak to graduate faculty and academic counselors in your university. These professionals usually can guide you to the right licensing information and resources.

3. Study for the appropriate licensing exam. Not every state uses the same national licensing exam. However, the two most common exams are the National Counselor Examination for Licensure and Certification (NCE) and the National Clinical Mental Health Counseling Examination (NCMHCE).

- The National Board for Certified Counselors has an easy map to determine the right exam for your counseling field based on your state here.
- The NCE is the appropriate examination for the National Certified Counselor (NCC) certification. Both exams are used to determine eligibility for military health systems such as TRICARE and the Army Substance Abuse Program.
- You can find study guides as well as test prep programs for each test as well.

4. Complete the required practice hours. Most counseling license requirements include a minimum number of supervised practice hours. The actual hours and nature of the practicum varies by the type of counseling and locality.

- To become licensed as a drug and alcohol counselor in New Jersey, for example, licensing applicants must have delivered 300 hours of counseling in functions ranging from client screening and orientation to treatment planning, counseling, and crisis intervention. Many other states require as many as 3,000 hours of supervised experience via an internship or residency.

5. Take the appropriate licensing exam. Once you've met your state's supervised practice requirements, you are ready to take the appropriate exam. The length and scoring of exams varies, but the NCE, for instance, is 200 multiple choice questions. It will cover various areas, including:

- Human growth and development
- Social and cultural diversity
- Helping relationships
- Group work
- Career development

- Assessment
- Research and program evaluation
- Professional orientation and ethical practice
- Fundamental counseling issues
- Counseling process
- Diagnostic and assessment services
- Professional practice
- Professional development, supervision, and consultation

6. Submit a counseling license application. Once you've completed all the necessary pieces of your state's specific licensing requirements, you will need to show proof to the responsible state board. Applications generally ask for documentation of academic credentials, test scores, and practice hours. In most cases, a processing fee is required.

- You can find a complete list of each state's licensing board here.
- Some states may also require you to schedule a time to appear before the board for an interview as well.

7. Maintain your counseling license by complying with local requirements. You may be required to enroll in workshops and seminars or take additional academic courses to maintain your license.

How to Maintain Confidentiality in Counseling

Confidentiality is an essential part of the counseling relationship. A client must be able to trust that the personal information he or she shares with you will not be revealed to other people. To protect their professional relationships, a counselor must explain the benefits and problems inherent in counseling services and clarify the limits of confidentiality to the client. Importantly, counselors have their own set of professional obligations which vary slightly from those of other mental health providers and which will vary from state to state.

Method 1. Explaining Confidentiality

1. Provide informed consent. To give informed consent, the counselor must explain the benefits and risks of counseling as well as its alternatives. They must also explain state laws regarding when they may be required to break confidentiality and describe how they might be required to do so. The counselor must request permission to record counseling sessions in writing or via video and audio. Counselors have a wide range of issues they should raise during a discussion of informed consent.

- These include the purposes, goals, techniques, and limitations of counseling.
- The counselors should discuss their qualifications, their credentials, their relevant experience, their approach to counseling and provisions for continuation of service should the counselor become unavailable to continue treatment.
- You should also explain fees, billing, and procedures in case of nonpayment.
- If any supervisors or peers will review records, this should be noted in the informed consent procedure.

2. Explain protection procedures. To obtain informed consent you need to explain how you will protect confidentiality. This includes detailing how records will be stored. It also includes explaining cases in which the client's comments are not confidential.

- This applies to electronic communications as well, including after hour phone calls, text messages, email, and skype sessions. You should discuss how confidentiality shall be maintained in such circumstances, and what risks to client confidentiality emerge when you are contacted after hours.

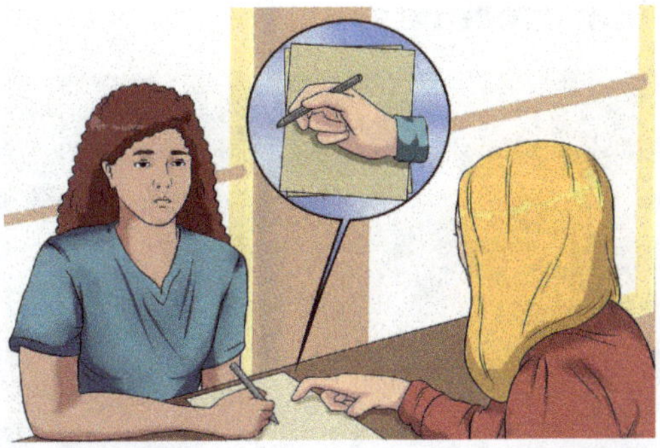

3. Give the patient a form to sign. You should provide a written form for the patient to sign, authorizing informed consent. This should remain in your patient's file. The language of the form is subject to change, but it should be inviting and easy to read. It should also cover most of the aforementioned points.

- It is advisable that you keep a copy of the form in the lobby so that patients can read it before speaking to you.

4. Get parental permission for minors. When counseling those under 18, informed consent must

come from a parent. You should have two separate forms, one informed consent form that the minor signs and another consent for treatment of minors form that the parent signs.

5. Describe research. If the sessions will be the basis for published research, this should be disclosed to the patient. Whether or not they will be anonymous and how their anonymity will be protected must be discussed.

Method 2. Protecting Client Records

1. Store records safely. To maintain confidentiality, it is the counselor's responsibility to keep the client's records safe and appropriately secured. Records should be locked away where only the counselor can reach them.

2. Protect records at home. It is important that you lock away documents at home as well as at the

office. However, you might need to step away from your desk or take an emergency phone call with others around. You should ensure that anyone you reside with is aware of confidentiality procedures.

- You should inform anyone with whom you reside what areas are off limits.
- You should also make it clear to anyone around when a phone call is confidential. Close the door and inform them that they should leave you alone.

3. Provide records to client. A client may request his or her own records in most situations. The counselor however can refuse to provide access to portions of the records if it will cause harm to the client. The counselor must document the request of the client and the reason for withholding the information.

- When there are multiple clients, such as with family counselling, then the counselor should only provide records relevant to the individual client, not other clients in the group.

4. Do not release records to any third parties. A client's records are only to be released to a third party if the client has provided written consent. This includes third parties who pay for treatment.

- With minors it is important to also obtain consent from parents before releasing information to a third party.

5. Be aware of exceptions. There are some exceptions when confidentiality should not be preserved. These vary somewhat with state law. You should make both yourself and your clients aware of these exceptions. Generally there are a few standards for the lapse of confidentiality:

- Confidentiality is waived when the client makes threats of suicide or homicide.
- It is also waived when information is disclosed relevant to the abuse of children or the elderly.
- Depending on the state in which you operate, you might be required to reveal to a third party when your client has a life-threatening disease that could be communicated to said third party.
- If a court subpoenas your records you should ask for written consent from your client. If that is not forthcoming, it is your responsibility to try to limit or prevent the disclosure of records.

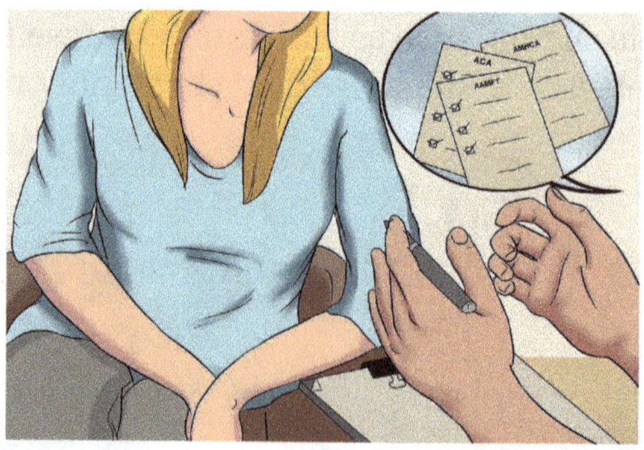

6. Stay current with counseling ethics and regulations. Counseling associations such as the American Association of Marriage and Family Therapists (AAMFT), the American Counseling Association (ACA)and the American Mental Health Counselors Association (AMHCA) all provide their members with a set of ethics for conducting counseling which include how to maintain confidentiality in a therapeutic relationship. You should also familiarize yourself with state regulations.

- When a counselor finds him or herself in a situation where maintaining a client's confidentiality becomes a problem, consulting with colleagues and a direct supervisor can help the counselor with appropriate decision-making.
- A counselor may also discuss confidentiality concerns with his or her own therapist, so long as they don't reveal information that may identify the client being discussed.

Method 3. Protecting Against Lapses in Conversations

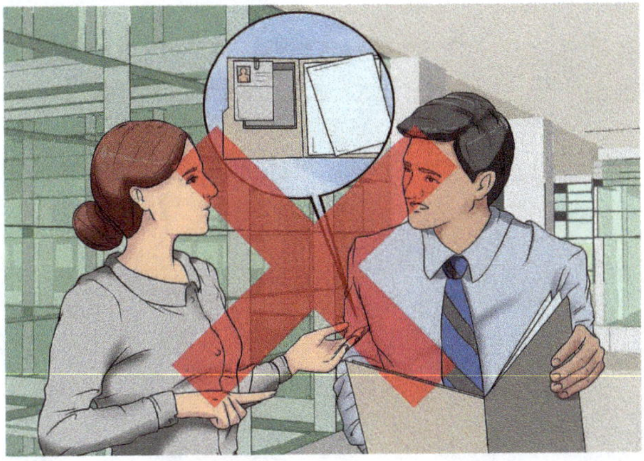

1. Avoid confidential details in discussions with peers. When a counselor seeks advice from a fellow professional about a client, they should not disclose confidential information. Information that is provided should not allow for the identification of the client. Furthermore, it should be limited to what is necessary to obtain relevant suggestions.

2. Change details. When engaged in conversation with friends or family, change important information about clients. Alter facts so that the client will be in no way identifiable.

3. Do not engage in conversations in public. All conversations about clients should be in a private

setting. If you receive an urgent phone call from a client, try to find a private place from which to return the call.

4. Do not acknowledge clients in public. Clients might not want their association with you to be public knowledge. Do not acknowledge them, unless they acknowledge you first.

Grief Counseling

Grief counseling is a form of psychotherapy that aims to help people cope with the physical, emotional, social, spiritual, and cognitive responses to loss. These experiences are commonly thought to be brought on by a loved person's death, but may more broadly be understood as shaped by any significant life-altering loss (e.g., divorce, home foreclosure, or job loss).

Grief counselors believe that everyone experiences and expresses grief in personally unique ways that are shaped by family background, culture, life experiences, personal values, and intrinsic beliefs. They believe that it is not uncommon for a person to withdraw from their friends and family and feel helpless; some might be angry and want to take action. Some may laugh while others experience strong regrets or guilt. Tears or the lack of crying can both be seen as appropriate expressions of grief.

Grief counselors know that one can expect a wide range of emotion and behavior associated with grief. Some counselors believe that in virtually all places and cultures, the grieving person benefits from the support of others. Further, grief counselors believe that where such support is lacking, counseling may provide an avenue for healthy resolution. Grief counselors also believe that where the process of grieving is interrupted, for example, by the one who is grieving having to simultaneously deal with practical issues of survival or by their having to be the strong one who is striving to hold their family together, grief can remain unresolved and later resurface as an issue for counseling.

Counseling

Grief counseling becomes necessary when a person is so disabled by their grief; and, so overwhelmed by their loss that their normal coping processes are disabled or shut down. Grief counseling facilitates expression of emotion and thought about the loss, including their feeling sad, anxious, angry, lonely, guilty, relieved, isolated, confused, or numb.

It includes thinking creatively about the challenges that follow loss and coping with concurrent changes in their lives. Often people feel disorganized, tired, have trouble concentrating, sleep poorly and have vivid dreams, and they may experience the change in appetite. These too are addressed in counseling.

Grief counseling facilitates the process of resolution in the natural reactions to loss. It is appropriate for reaction to losses that have overwhelmed a person's coping ability. There are considerable resources online covering grief or loss counseling such as the Grief Counseling Resource Guide from the New York State Office of Mental Health.

Grief counseling may be called upon when a person suffers anticipatory grief, for example, an intrusive and frequent worry about a loved one whose death is neither imminent nor likely. Anticipatory mourning also occurs when a loved one has a terminal illness. This can handicap that person's ability to stay present whilst simultaneously holding onto, letting go of, and drawing closer to the dying relative.

Joanne Jozefowski in 1999 through The Phoenix Phenomenon: Rising from the Ashes of Grief summarizes five stages to rebuild a shattered life:

- Impact: shock, denial, anxiety, fear, and panic.
- Chaos: confusion, disbelief, actions out of control, irrational thoughts and feelings, feeling despair, feeling helpless, desperate searching, lose track of time, difficulty sleeping and eating, obsessive focus on the loved one and their possessions, agony from imagining their physical harm, shattered beliefs.
- Adapting: bringing order back into daily life while you continue to grieve: take care of basic needs (personal grooming, shopping, cooking, cleaning, paying bills), learn to live without the loved one, accept help, focus on helping children cope, connect with other grieving families for mutual support, take control of grieving so that grief does not control you, slowly accept the new reality.
- Equilibrium: attaining stability and routines: reestablish a life that works all right, enjoy pleasant activities with family members and good times with friends, do productive work, choose a positive new direction in life while honoring the past, learn how to handle people who ask questions about what you've been through.
- Transformation: rethinking your purpose in life and the basis for your identity; looking for meaning in tragic, senseless loss; allowing yourself to have both painful and positive feelings about your loss and become able to choose which feelings you focus on; allowing yourself to discover that your struggle has led you to develop a stronger, better version of yourself than you expected could exist; learning how to talk with others about your heroic healing journey without exposing them to your pain; becoming supportive of others trying to deal with their losses.

Grief Therapy

There is a distinction between grief counseling and grief therapy. Counseling involves helping people move through uncomplicated, or normal, grief to health and resolution. Grief therapy involves the use of clinical tools for traumatic or complicated grief reactions. This could occur where the grief reaction is prolonged or manifests itself through some bodily or behavioral symptom, or by a grief response outside the range of cultural or psychiatrically defined normality.

Grief therapy is a kind of psychotherapy used to treat severe or complicated traumatic grief reactions, which are usually brought on by the loss of a close person (by separation or death) or by community disaster. The goal of grief therapy is to identify and solve the psychological and emotional problems which appeared as a consequence.

They may appear as behavioral or physical changes, psychosomatic disturbances, delayed or extreme mourning, conflictual problems or sudden and unexpected mourning). Grief therapy may be available as individual or group therapy. A common area where grief therapy has been extensively applied is with the parents of cancer patients.

Controversies

Efficacy and Iatrogenesis

At present, a controversy exists in the scholarly literature regarding grief therapy's relative efficacy and the possible harm from it (iatrogenesis). Researchers have suggested that people may resort to receiving grief therapy in the absence of complicated (or abnormal) grief reactions and that, in such cases, grief therapy may cause a normal bereavement response to turn pathological. Others have argued that grief therapy is highly effective for people who suffer from unusually prolonged and complicated responses to bereavement.

A particular research lists grief counseling and grief therapy among the treatment with the potential on a list of treatments with the potential to cause harm to clients. In particular, individuals experiencing "relatively normal bereavement reactions" were said to be at risk of a worse outcome after receiving grief counselling.

Validity of "Complicated Grief"

Some mental health professionals have questioned whether complicated grief exists. New diagnostic criteria for "complicated grief" have been proposed for the new DSM, the DSM-V. One argument against creating a classification for "complicated grief" holds that it is not a unique mental disorder. Rather it is a combination of other mental disorders, such as depression, posttraumatic stress disorder, and personality disorders.

Empirical studies have been attempting to convincingly establish the incremental validity of complicated grief. In 2007, George Bonanno and colleagues published a paper describing a study that supports the incremental validity of complicated grief. The paper cautions, "the question of how complicated grief symptoms might be organized diagnostically is still very much open to debate."

As this is a current debate in the field, new research on this topic is likely to appear in the scientific literature.

Trauma Counseling

Anticipating the impact of loss or trauma (to the extent than anyone can), and during and after the events of loss or trauma, each person has unique emotional experiences and ways of coping, of grieving and of reacting or not. Sudden, violent or unexpected loss or trauma imposes additional strains on coping. When a community is affected such as by disaster both the cost and sometimes the supports are greater.

Weeping, painful feelings of sadness, anger, shock, guilt, helplessness and outrage are not uncommon. These are particularly challenging times for children who may have had little experience managing strong affects within themselves or in their family. These feelings are all part of a natural healing process that draws on the resilience of the person, family and community.

Time and the comfort and support of understanding loved ones and once strangers who come to their aid, supports people healing in their own time and their own way. Research shows that resilience is ordinary rather than extraordinary. The majority of people who survive loss and trauma do not go on to develop PTSD. Some remain overwhelmed.

This topic addresses counseling with complex grief and trauma, not only complex post-traumatic stress disorder but those conditions of traumatic loss and psychological trauma that for a number of reasons are enduring or disabling. For example, where an adult is periodically immobilised by unwelcome and intrusive recall of the sudden and violent death of a parent in their childhood.

One that they were unable to grieve because they were the strong one who held the family together, or whose feelings of outrage and anger were unacceptable or unmanageable at the time or because the loss of the breadwinner catapulted the family into a precipitous fall losing home, community and means of support.

Post-trauma Self

Because of the interconnectedness of trauma, PTSD, human development, resiliency and the integration of the self, counseling of the complex traumatic aftermath of a violent death in the family, for example, require an integrative approach, using a variety of skills and techniques to best fit the presentation of the problem.

Disruption in the previously supportive bonds of attachment and of the person's ability to manage their own affects challenges traditional, so called 'non-directive' client centered counseling approaches. One example of this paradigm shift in approaches is the Multitheoretical Psychotherapy of Jeff Brooks-Harris.

The post-traumatic self may not be the same person as before. This can be the source of shame, secondary shocks after the event and of grief for the lost unaltered self, which impacts on family and work. Counseling in these circumstances is designed to maximize safety, trauma processing, and reintegration regardless of the specific treatment approach.

How to do Grief Counseling

Everyone experiences grief differently and there is no one way to help a person suffering from grief. Instead of trying to impose your own vision of what the grieving person needs, you should be there to offer companionship, a shoulder to cry on, and emotional validation. He will need to spend time grieving. You should tell him that his feelings are natural and encourage him to find his own way of commemorating his loved one.

Part 1. Practicing Helpful Counseling Techniques

1. Act as a companion. Each person's experience with grief is different. That means that no level of expertise will equip you to tell the person in mourning how he should respond. Your role is to provide company, listen, and validate their feelings.

- Don't tell, listen.
- Constantly reinforce that their response is normal and natural.
- Encourage them to use their own skills to cope with grief. If they are an artist, encourage them to use this ability to express his feelings.
- Help them understand and recognize their feelings.
- Help them develop a schedule that allows them to manage their daily tasks while reducing unnecessary outside stressors.
- Remember that your job is to be there, not to take away the pain. That is impossible. Your job is to support them, not to try to fix them.

2. Validate feelings. It is important to make it clear that you understand the person's feelings. Be

sure that they know that such feelings are natural and that people experience grief differently. It might be useful to explain some of the common responses to grief and make it clear that they are natural.

- Those who experience instrumental grief focus on problem solving and try to control emotional responses.
- Those who experience intuitive grieving have intense emotional experiences that might include depression and thoughts about mortality.
- It is common for people to blame themselves, feel anger, hopelessness, anxiety, and withdrawal from the world.

3. Ask open questions. Don't ask leading questions or "yes" and "no" questions. Ask big, broad questions, that encourage him to think about his feelings and explore the subjects that he is interested in. Make it clear that you want to know what he feels, but are not questioning the validity of his feelings.

- Do not ask "why" questions. These make it sound as if you do not understand or support his feelings.
- Ask broad questions like "How do you feel."
- Ask "What bothers you the most."
- Instead of asking "Why do you feel that way?" ask "Could you give me specific examples."

4. Paraphrase responses. When you are trying to get to the core of her problems, try giving a short

summary of what you think she has told you. This will demonstrate that you are listening and might help her get a better grip on what is bothering her the most.

- If she tells you, "I stay up every night thinking about him. When I go to work I am tired and can't think clearly. I am getting more and more nervous and depressed because I can't function during the day." Ask, "So your grief is causing sleep problems that disrupt your life?"

5. Reflect his feelings. When you get a sense for how he feels, verify that you have correctly understood his emotions. This is a way to demonstrate that you are listening and that you have developed an emotional connection.

- Try, "Sounds like you are very angry about what has happened."
- Alternatively, "It sounds like you are having difficulty understanding your emotions."

6. Refrain from unsupportive behavior. Everything you do should be directed at her. Anything that suggests your focus is elsewhere will be counterproductive. You should avoid forcing your own solutions upon her.

- Do not watch the clock.

- Do not take notes.
- Do not look around the room.
- Do not try to read too much into her feelings and impose your own idea or her feelings on her.
- Do not preach about what she should do.
- Refrain from giving too much advice or asking too many questions.
- Do not respond too quickly. Allow moments of silence.
- Do not change the subject.
- Do not talk too much about yourself.

Part 2. Developing a Supportive Personal

1. Look him in the eye. Look him in the eye to show that you are interested in and engaged with what he is saying. Allow your face to demonstrate that you are emotional and supportive. Be dynamic and engaged, possibly nodding in affirmation.

2. Keep your body open and relaxed. Crossed legs and arms may suggest that you are closed off or uninviting. Try to sit straight up, with your limbs open. Your body should appear relaxed and you can gesture with your hands to show emotional support.

- Also be sure that your body is facing directly toward the grieving person to indicate that you are engaged with her.
- Sit on the same level as the person you are talking to. Do not take a chair that allows you to tower over her, or her over you. This creates a sense of power imbalance that is not helpful for open conversation.

3. Talk like you care. Talk naturally and allow your voice to show emotion. Try to develop a soothing tone in your voice. Your conversation style should also demonstrate that you are there to listen. Don't interrupt him, go from topic to topic, or rush him to an answer.

- It is okay to leave periods of silence. These allow him to think about his feelings and ensure that he does not feel that he has been cut off or is rushed to respond.

Part 3. Using Rituals for Remembrance

1. Get her to plan ahead for important dates. Holidays or important dates in the person's relationship with the person she lost can trigger feelings of loss. Encourage her to plan ahead to commemorate those days. This can help her create a feeling of continuity with the past or create the sense that you are moving on.

- While it is particularly useful to develop a ritual for special dates, there is no reason why the griever shouldn't plan to celebrate or remember the deceased any other day.

2. Encourage him to commemorate with ritual. There is a plethora of rituals he can use to remember his loved lost one. Which one he picks depends on his relationship with the person and what it was that once brought them together. Some examples include:

- Preparing a meal that the deceased enjoyed.
- Watch a movie that the person enjoyed.
- Go on a walk, possibly where the two of had been in the past, and remember times spent together.
- Buy flowers on important days.
- Travel somewhere the deceased wanted to go.
- Listen to music that reminds the grieving person of the deceased.
- Look through a photo album.

3. Encourage her to express his grief through art. Ask her to write fiction, personal essays, or poetry that expresses and identifies feelings and blockages. You can encourage artists to paint or draw. Starting a journal can be an important step for dealing with emotions.

- Ask her to try writing about the life of the person she lost.
- Alternatively, have her write about how that person has influenced her. Remind her that the deceased lives on through her.

4. Create a memory book. Memory books can help in the grieving process. Compile mementos, photos or stories about the deceased person. This helps one come to terms with the magnitude of the loss and to focus on the realities of one's new life without forgetting the lost loved one.

5. Use the open-chair technique. Place an open chair opposite the grieving person and ask her to imagine the deceased person sitting in that chair. Give the bereaved person the opportunity to speak to the person in the chair and say all the things that she would like to have said to that person.

- Playing out situations from the past or rehearsing difficult future situations may help bring closure.
- The use of objects and memorabilia, such as jewelry and other objects which the bereaved person is comfortable with, can be used to facilitate talking and bringing the mourning process to a close.

6. Don't push. Some people will want to clear their heads or process their loss before trying to commemorate their loved one. Many people have difficulty talking about what has happened. It is your job to give the grieving party ideas about how to move on. It is not your job to force them to do something they do not want to do.

CHAPTER 3 Mental Health Treatments

Mental disorders are defined as psychological conditions that are characterized by disorganization of the mind, personality and emotions to that extent so as to impair significantly the normal psychological and social functioning of an individual. The treatments of these conditions include psychotherapy and medications, such as anti-depressants and anti-psychotics. The diverse mental health treatments for treating depression during pregnancy, anxiety disorder, delusional disorder, bipolar disorder, postpartum psychosis, social anxiety, schizophrenia, etc. have been extensively discussed in this chapter.

How to Treat Depression During Pregnancy

Expecting a child is usually associated with joy and delight. That is why some women are shocked and confused when what they feel instead is sadness and melancholy. Depression during pregnancy is not that uncommon and even though it makes a challenging period of life even more difficult for the mother-to-be, the good news is that it can be treated very successfully. There are many ways to treat this problem; find one that suits your preferences best or combine all of them. Whatever you decide to do, taking immediate action is what matters the most.

Part 1. Changing your Daily Routine

1. Plan and structure your day. Depression should not determine your schedule. When it does, you avoid social interaction and productivity and, as a result, you keep on rolling in its negative cycle. Try to make your day full and full of useful and handy activities to stay busy and to accomplish tasks to give you encouragement. Staying busy and productive is one of the best ways to help to alleviate depression.

- Routines can help, too. As humans, we like feeling safe and knowing what to expect – which is exactly what having a routine can do. Have rituals that you can rely on every day whether it's lunch with a friend, yoga, cooking dinner, or a bath. This is time you know your brain can slow down.

2. Make time for the things you enjoy. When you're planning your busy day, be sure to always make time for your favorite activities. This will boast your motivation and will lift up your mood. Don't feel guilty about that movie. It's now more than ever before that you deserve adequate time to be happy.

- If you catch yourself feeling guilty for getting that pedicure or scheduling in an hour-long bath, remember that being a mom is a 24/7 job. In time, you won't have time for you. This is just you getting everything on your to-do list out of the way while you can.

3. Make regular exercise a priority. Just like bright lights, exercising and sexual activity release two hormones that make you feel joyful – dopamine and endorphins. These hormones are responsible for feelings such as euphoria, excess energy and hopefulness. These are all very important to experience throughout your entire life, but especially during pregnancy. Naturally, you don't have to exercise vigorously. Pilates, yoga, and other similar exercises are both very suitable during a pregnancy.

- Apart from helping your body release those "happy" hormones and thus fight depression, exercise will help you keep to your initial weight. Very often pregnant women become depressed because of the body changes they endure, thus making them feel unattractive. Workouts, even light ones, will help you feel fit and strong and will therefore soothe the sense of being depressed.

- Nevertheless, before starting on any exercise routine at all, make sure to talk things over with your obstetrician, as he or she can tell you what specific workouts are suitable in your case.

4. Make relaxing a priority, too. Being pregnant can be a highly stressful, anxiety-ridden time. This sets you up for depression, especially when you're under the impression you should be overjoyed with your current situation and aren't. Two things you can do to combat the stress? Meditation and naps.

- Meditation can lower your cortisol levels which lowers your stress, making you sleep better and ultimately feel happier. So when you don't quite have time to meet up for virgin cocktails with the girls, try spending that free time meditating. Even just 15 minutes of zen can make a difference.
- Naps, on the other hand, mean more sleep, which helps you feel more energized and balanced. Just try to keep them to an hour or less so you don't mess up your sleep schedule.

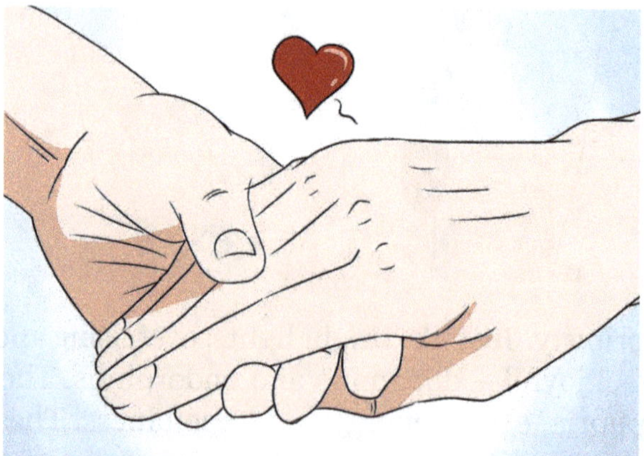

5. Join a support group. Women suffering with depression during pregnancy is not an uncommon issue. Most of the women you know have either gone through it themselves or know someone who has. While having friends and family at your side is invaluable, having a support group of women going through the same thing can help you realize just how not alone you are.

- Talk to your friends, family, coworkers, or even doctor about resources. Your hospital may either offer a program or know of a women's organization that does. If you're currently in therapy, your psychologist may have some ideas, too. And, as always, the Internet is full of resources, too.

Part 2. Taking Control of your Emotions

1. Surround yourself with loved ones. If you are experiencing depression, talking about your feelings to friends and family can be very useful. They won't necessary be able to give you any advice, but the fact that they are there and are willing to hear everything you need to say is usually enough to make you feel loved and less isolated.

- Depression during pregnancy is often caused by relationship problems, worries about the future and anxiety concentrated around the much expected baby. In addition, it is a well-known fact that women have more in-depth experiences while they are pregnant, due to hormonal imbalance. So, even though support from others is generally an important factor of human life, it is especially essential during a woman's pregnancy.

2. Be open about how you're feeling. It is very important to know that you have people to count on. However, what's more important is to actually count on them. More often than not, depression is caused by feelings like loneliness – asking for help when you need it can make you feel infinitely better.

- Carrying a child changes your mind and body in a lot of ways and that might sometimes make you feel misunderstood, scared and isolated from everybody else. This is why support is a key part of dealing with depression during pregnancy – if you ask for help when you need it, your loved ones can help these miserable feelings disappear. What's more, your mom/sisters/cousins/friends may have been right there too.

- Even if currently you don't feel much support from your loved ones, you should explain to them why you need it – keep in mind that they have no way of knowing what is going on in your mind and need to be told that their help is required.

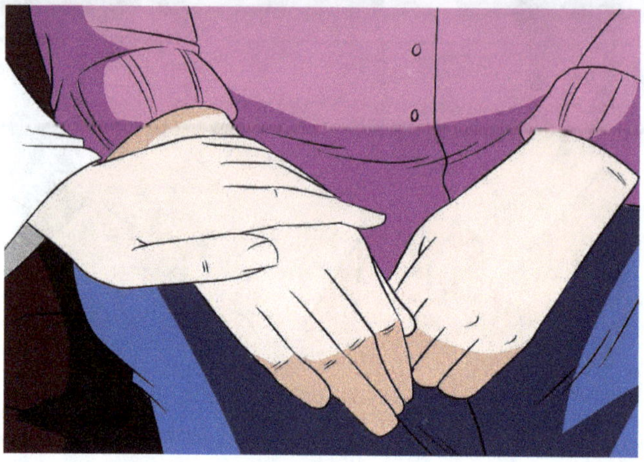

3. Try to forgive and forget more often. Often in depression we fail to forgive ourselves and others over minor mistakes. We are being cruel to ourselves and others needlessly. Try to accept things with an open heart. No one is perfect and rigid thinking is never helpful. Healing comes through forgiveness and letting go.

- Pregnant women often find themselves being moody and irritable for no reason. They see themselves nagging and being hurtful when they know inside they don't mean it – it's just the hormones talking. Those around you know that you're at the whim of your mood swings, so forgive yourself too. Not just those around you.

4. Identify the negative thoughts that cause you problems. Underlying core negative thoughts (also known as negative automatic thoughts) often remain unrecognized. This is pivotal as they are the main source of depressive rumination. Identify these thoughts, write them down and practice replacing them with positive ones.

- When you catch yourself thinking, "Life has never been good to me," stop for a second. After that thought, think to yourself, "No, that's not right. Though there have been hard times, life has also given me happiness and pleasure."
- Try to omit should and musts from your life. Don't demand excessively from yourself, environment or others. This will help you a lot.

5. Make your tool kit for better coping. These consist of small coping cards, on which you have written positive statements for yourself. Here are some ideas:

- You can make coping cards using colorful paper, charts or any other material. Cut it in small cards and write positive and forceful statements that help you change and cope with negativity. For example, "I have always coped well and I have the strength to do it again."
- Cue cards can be pasted anywhere in your room and whenever you start feeling depressed or start thinking negatively, they can remind you to stop. They are very helpful in distracting and reducing cycles of negative thoughts.
- Make your activity schedule on an A4 sheet or card and paste it on your cupboard or nearby place. Daily, mark the activities you have performed to check your progress. This is very helpful in dealing with depression and will give you insight regarding your progress and will motivate you to further action.

6. Remember to live in the present. Living in the past, constantly thinking about negative events

does not allow to focus on the present. Enjoy today, focus on what you have and try to live in the here and now. You're about to bring a life into the world.

- Living in the future is almost as bad. Constantly worrying about how you'll make ends meet or what kind of mother you'll be will get you nowhere. The fact that you're worrying at all means you care – which is the first step. Focusing on what you can do now to improve the present will also improve the future.

Part 3. Changing your Sleeping Patterns

1. Take charge of the way you sleep by creating a sleep schedule. One of the most widespread symptoms of depression is sleep disturbance – getting either too much or too little sleep. Sleep is an important part of staying mentally healthy and when you don't get the right amount, mood swings and depression are often the result. To avoid these negative consequences, prepare a sleep schedule.

- Coming up with a sleep schedule depends on your personal needs – some people need to sleep more than others. However, when depression during pregnancy is concerned, the generally accepted rule is that you should sleep about 9 hours per night, and have two short naps during the day (approximately an hour long for each).

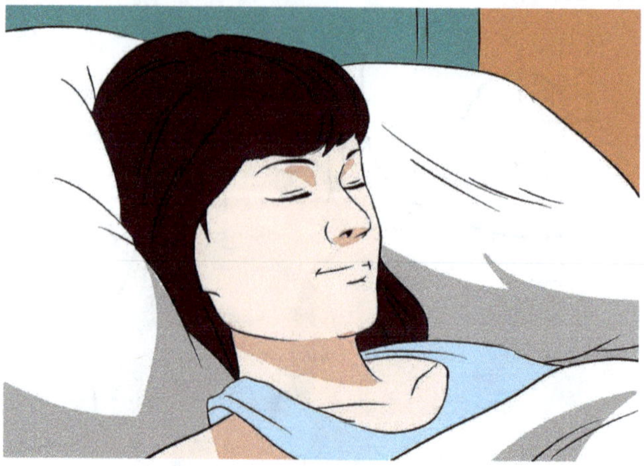

2. Go to sleep and wake up at the same time each day and night. To reap the benefits of your sleep

schedule, you're going to need to go to sleep and wake up every night and morning at the same time. It's best to have it at the same time every night so your body can get used to the schedule and eventually find it easier to sleep.

- This will mean some sacrifices, yes. If you choose 10 PM as the time to go to sleep, this includes weekends, too. There will be the occasional night when you want to stay up (or morning when you want to sleep in), but the schedule still needs adhering to.

3. Observe your sleep schedule strictly. This might be difficult to do at first, and it is very likely that the first few times you will toss and turn without being able to fall asleep, but in a few days your body will get used to the new regime and things will get easier.

- Depression itself usually also affects your sleep. The biggest problem with this symptom is that it feeds a vicious cycle. In order to get yourself out of this sleeping trap and feel happier, you need to dedicate yourself to this idea of a sleep schedule and stick to it. Normalcy and routine are key.

4. If you get off your schedule, take a nap. Sleep is especially important when suffering from depression during pregnancy because it is what allows your brain to fully rest and recharge. As your brain is the organ that controls your emotions, and therefore depression, depriving it from the right amount of sleep can be very harmful. If you spend a night tossing and turning, make up for it with a nap during the day.

- Two one-hour naps are appropriate during pregnancy if you did not receive enough sleep the night before. However, be sure that these naps don't interfere with you falling asleep and waking up on time the next day.

Part 4. Treating Depression through Therapy

1. Try Cognitive Behavioral Therapy (CBT) to change your thinking. CBT is a type of psychotherapy which has shown very positive effects on conditions such as depression. However, when it comes to pregnancy, CBT is very useful even if you are not feeling depressed, as it will help you accept and understand your new situation better and can truly prepare you for the new joy in your life – the baby.

- This approach has been constructed around the belief that our thoughts influence our actions and therefore negative thoughts result in negative actions.
- However, this therapy is not simply a "positive thinking" approach; it goes much deeper than that. CBT examines the thoughts that you tend to have and helps you build a positive outlook on life, which is incredibly useful when it comes to fighting depression.
- Negative thoughts, such as "Why does this always happen to me?", result in negative experiences and behaviors, such as falling victim to depression. That is why CBT aims to transform negative thoughts into positive and more realistic ones, such as "Yes, this situation isn't the easiest one, but instead of feeling defeated, what can I do to feel happy?"

2. Turn to CBT to prepare you for your child, too. CBT can also be very helpful when preparing you for the arrival of your child as this life event, as exciting as it is, can also be very stressful and

overwhelming and could, in itself, be the cause of depression. In these cases your therapist will help you find the deeper meaning behind thoughts such as "I am afraid I won't be a good mother" and transform them to healthier views such as "Everyone makes mistakes and I will probably make some too with my child, but that's OK because I will always do my best to be a great parent."

- As we mentioned above, depression during pregnancy is often the result of relationship problems or an inability to understand and accept the new situation you are in. CBT can be really useful here because it finds the underlying reasons for your problems and helps you turn things around.

3. Try bright light therapy. This depression treatment approach is relatively new, but it does hold promise and it is safe for pregnant and breastfeeding women. This type of therapy is especially useful in the winter season, or when your condition will not allow you to expose your skin to sunlight for too long.

- Basically, bright light therapy means exposure to very bright lights, using a special light box (simple home lighting is not enough) at illumination level of 10,000 lux, most commonly for 30 to 40 minutes.
- The operating principle of this therapy is based on the fact that our body works in an interesting way – light stimulates it to release hormones that make you feel happy and even euphoric.

4. Alternatively, spend more time outside. If your living situation allows it, you can choose the

natural way – spend more time in the sun and in nature. The scientific explanation behind this interesting phenomena is that people are able to function best during the day and are very dependent on the warmth of the sun. That is why over time our brains have adapted to seek light and to ensure that we do that, we have evolved to feel pleasure when exposed to it.

- Even though bright light therapy has not yet be proven successful in all depression sufferers, it does help over half of the people who try it, as was discovered by a study conducted by the Medical Psychiatry in 2005. So, if you are a pregnant woman suffering from depression, give it a try.

Part 5. Understanding Pregnancy and Depression

1. Know the common symptoms of depression during pregnancy. These will help you understand your own condition and what areas you might want to address in order to treat your depression. The common symptoms of depression during pregnancy include the following:

- Disturbed appetite (increased or decreased)
- Disturbed sleep (increased or decreased)
- Extreme fatigue and loss of energy
- Crying spells
- Poor fetal attachment
- Lack of feelings of pleasure
- Irritability
- Suicidal ideation
- Thoughts and feelings of worthlessness

2. Identify the risk factors. There are some common factors that enhance the risk of depression and if addressed timely might alleviate prenatal depression. These factors include:

- Dysfunctional thinking and coping styles with ongoing life stressors.
- Problems with significant relationships in family.
- Current negative/stressful life events.
- History of physical, emotional or sexual abuse.
- Earlier miscarriage or stillbirth.
- Childbirth related distress.
- Vulnerable personality type to depression and anxiety.
- If these factors existed prior to pregnancy, know that there is a greater chance of an ongoing depression and functional coping is required to treat it.

3. Know that you're not alone. Depression during pregnancy can be a very scary and startling experience. Most mothers expect to be overwhelmed with joy all the time, though that is hardly the case. Keep in mind that this is a trying time for both your body and your psyche and the healthiest way to deal with things is to seek help and support as soon as you feel you might be depressed.

- Slightly over 1 in 10 women experience depression during or after pregnancy. You are hardly alone. Talk to the women in your family or your friends – odds are one of them has been there, too.

How to Screen for Depression During Pregnancy

It's estimated that between 14-23% of pregnant women struggle with symptoms of depression. During pregnancy, many hormonal changes occur, which can directly affect symptoms of depression and anxiety. Coupled with situational stressors, depression can occur during pregnancy. While some women experience moodiness during pregnancy, it's important to address any potential depression so that you can properly treat it.

Part 1. Identifying Symptoms of Depression

1. Examine physical symptoms. Indications of depression can include several physical symptoms. It's important to determine whether your symptoms are typical of pregnancy or if they seem more extreme or enduring for longer. If you've suffered from some of the following symptoms more days than not for two or more weeks in a way that affects your normal functioning, it may be related to depression:

- Decreased energy/feeling constantly exhausted
- Feeling restless; fidgeting often
- Feeling overly lethargic or making slow movements

2. Look at possible emotional symptoms of depression. Pregnancy often affects emotions, and it's

important to differentiate between emotional changes that are part of a normal pregnancy and those that may be due to depression. Check to see if you have had emotional symptoms of depression for two or more weeks that have affected your functioning at home, school, or work. Emotional symptoms that may indicate that you have depression include:

- Feeling worthless
- Difficulty concentrating, problems with memory
- Persistent sadness, crying
- Low mood, feeling numb
- Feeling irritable, angry or aggressive
- Decreased interest in activities you used to enjoy
- Feeling unmotivated or detached from your typical routine
- Having thoughts of harming yourself or the baby

3. Recognize behavioral symptoms. You or other people may see changes in the way you act that differ from your normal behavior. While it's typical to experience some hormonal changes during pregnancy that can affect your behavior, it's important to determine whether your behavior changes are within the range of 'normal' or if they may be related to depression. If you notice behavior changes that impair your functioning and that last 2 or more weeks, it's time to consider depression. Behavioral symptoms can include:

- Changes in sleep habits (sleeping too much or too little, such as staying up all night or wanting to sleep all day even if you slept well at night)
- Changes in eating habits (beyond what may be considered "normal" in pregnancy, such as binge eating or not wanting to eat at all)
- Socially withdrawing from friends and family, isolating yourself
- Engaging in reckless behavior (like things that may harm the fetus, like drinking)

4. Ask yourself if there's a family or personal history of depression. Look at your family members and ask yourself if there's a family history of depression. Then, ask yourself whether you've previously experienced depression at any point in your life. If so, you are at a higher risk for developing depression.

- Does anyone in your immediate family (parents, siblings) suffer from depression or take medication to treat depression? What about your extended family (grandparents, aunts/uncles, cousins).
- Have you ever taken medication, seen a therapist, or struggled with symptoms of depression in the past.

Part 2. Screening Medical or Physical Contributions

1. Acknowledge physical discomforts. Dealing with the changes and pain from pregnancy can become wearing day after day. From morning sickness to back pain to minimal sleeping positions, the physical stress from pregnancy can deplete normal ability to cope and leave you drained and exhausted.

- Are you finding it more difficult to respond to stress due to the pain you experience regularly? Do you feel like you have a shorter fuse or that your discomfort is making you excessively sad or irritable? How is your pregnancy affecting your emotional state.
- Help your body relax by taking warm baths, using a heating pad for muscle aches, and using good posture.

2. Recognize problems in your pregnancy. If you're struggling with a high-risk pregnancy or have increased medical complications with your pregnancy, you may be at higher risk for depression. Dealing with stress and the fear of any problems with your baby can be too much to handle.You may also feel frustrated or unhelpful if you're not allowed to work or do things you could previously do with ease.

- Are you feeling worthless or unneeded in your family due to a complicated pregnancy? Are you bedridden and frustrated at your lack of independence? Are these issues affecting your emotional or mental health? These situations can contribute to depression.
- Make sure you stay in contact with your medical practitioner and communicate any questions you may have about your pregnancy.

3. Ask yourself if fertility treatments have affected your well-being. If you've endured several months of fertility treatments, it's likely that your body and emotions are under stress. Especially if you tried tirelessly to get pregnant and now are, you may be worried to lose the baby you tried so hard to conceive. The fertility process is a difficult one and emotionally taxing. Once you're pregnant, it can stay difficult. All of these factors can make you more prone to depression.

- Have you found it more difficult to manage your emotions since fertility treatments? How have the treatments and resulting stress from the treatments affecting your mental and emotional health.

- Think about the stressors your body, mind, and emotions have experienced during and after treatments. Find ways to express these feelings healthfully, such as through talking to a friend or a therapist.

Part 3. Expressing Emotional Factors

1. Acknowledge past pregnancy loss. A previous loss such as a miscarriage can impact your feelings about the current pregnancy. You may find yourself excessively worried about the baby and if it will survive. Acknowledge the loss and allow yourself to work through the grief and disappointment.

- Do you find yourself constantly worried about the baby's health? Have you fully healed from the past loss? Does this affect your own well-being and emotional health.
- If you've experienced a pregnancy loss, don't hesitate to reach out for help. Your friends and family want to support you. Talk about the baby and use the name. It's okay to acknowledge what would have or could have been.

2. Ask a friend. If you think you may be depressed, ask a friend to reflect back to you any changes to your emotional health that he or she has noticed. Ask someone you know will be honest with you, such as a sibling or best friend. Share how you've been feeling and if he or she has noticed changes in your behavior, emotions, or moods.

3. Seek therapy. If you have suspicions that you may be depressed during your pregnancy, seek a mental health professional. You can talk about your symptoms and how you feel. A therapist can give you a diagnosis and help emotionally support you through the pregnancy. She or he can help you find coping strategies to help lift the depression, help shift negative thoughts, give you tools to help adjust behaviors, and arm you with how to prevent future depression.

Part 4. Examining Home Life Difficulties

1. Examine relationship problems. If you're struggling with your romantic relationship with your partner, it can trigger depression. Some people try to stick it out and assume that having the baby will dissolve all the problems; it won't. The baby will only add strain to the relationship.

- Do you find yourself taking your stress out on your partner? Are issues between you and your partner more tumultuous than before you were pregnant? Think about how your relationship may have changed since becoming pregnant.
- Holding on to relationship stress can affect the growing fetus and increase the likelihood of the baby developing behavior problems in childhood. Let go of anger and resentment and work through relationship problems as quickly as possible.
- If your relationship is struggling, get counseling. Don't delay on getting the help you need. For more information, check out How to Tell if You Need to See a Therapist.

2. Deal with financial concerns. It's normal to be concerned about affording a new baby. However, financial difficulties may cause a significant amount of stress and contribute to depression. Before the baby comes, create a budget to help you feel more in control and reduce finance related stress.

- Try to make small changes to save money. For example, you can purchase generic items, watch for sales, clip coupons, buy frequently used items in bulk, or limit entertainment purchases, such as eating out or going to the movies.
- Consider DIY options to save money, such as making your own baby food or making reusable cloth diapers.
- Ask friends and family if they would be willing to help you with childcare after your baby is born. Friends and family members may also be willing to donate items to you such as baby clothes, a car seat, a baby monitor, or a stroller.

3. Acknowledge a past history of abuse. A history of abuse as a child may contribute to your risk of suffering from major depression as an adult. Abuse may take the form of sexual abuse, physical abuse, emotional abuse, and neglect. No matter what type of abuse you suffered as a child, it is important to seek help as an adult.

- If you were abused as a child, seek help from a therapist to work towards recovery.
- If you've experienced past abuse, check out How to Love Yourself After a Long Battle in an Abusive Relationship.
- If you're experiencing current abuse, please report it and seek help. See How to Leave an Abusive Relationship.

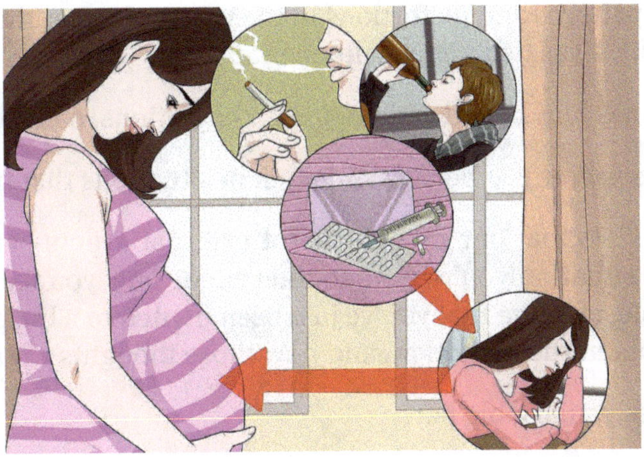

4. Look at major risk factors. If you are young, single, or have an unplanned pregnancy, you have a higher risk for depression. Other risk factors include a maternal age, lifestyle choices (like taking drugs, drinking alcohol, or smoking), medical history (like previous pregnancy complications), and carrying multiples. Think about how these factors may affect your well-being during pregnancy. You may need additional support during your pregnancy to avoid developing depression.

How to Treat Anxiety Disorder with Therapies

When it comes to treating anxiety disorders, research shows that therapy is usually the most effective option. That's because anxiety therapy—unlike anxiety medication—treats more than just the symptoms of the problem. Therapy can help you uncover the underlying causes of your worries and fears; learn how to relax; look at situations in new, less frightening ways; and develop better coping and problem-solving skills. Therapy gives you the tools to overcome anxiety and teaches you how to use them.

Anxiety disorders differ considerably, so therapy should be tailored to your specific symptoms and diagnosis. If you have obsessive-compulsive disorder (OCD), for example, your treatment will be different from someone who needs help for anxiety attacks. The length of therapy will also depend on the type and severity of your anxiety disorder. However, many anxiety therapies are relatively short-term. According to the American Psychological Association, many people improve significantly within 8 to 10 therapy sessions.

Many different types of therapy are used to treat anxiety, but the leading approaches are cognitive behavioral therapy (CBT) and exposure therapy. Each anxiety therapy may be used alone, or combined with other types of therapy. Anxiety therapy may be conducted individually, or it may take place in a group of people with similar anxiety problems.

Cognitive behavioral Therapy for Anxiety

Cognitive behavioral therapy (CBT) is the most widely-used therapy for anxiety disorders. Research has shown it to be effective in the treatment of panic disorder, phobias, social anxiety disorder, and generalized anxiety disorder, among many other conditions.

CBT addresses negative patterns and distortions in the way we look at the world and ourselves. As the name suggests, this involves two main components:

Cognitive therapy examines how negative thoughts, or cognitions, contribute to anxiety.

Behavior therapy examines how you behave and react in situations that trigger anxiety.

The basic premise of CBT is that our thoughts—not external events—affect the way we feel. In other words, it's not the situation you're in that determines how you feel, but your perception of the situation. For example, imagine that you've just been invited to a big party. Consider three different ways of thinking about the invitation, and how those thoughts would affect your emotions.

Situation: A friend invites you to a big party

Thought 1: The party sounds like a lot of fun. I love going out and meeting new people.

Emotions: Happy, excited

Thought 2: Parties aren't my thing. I'd much rather stay in and watch a movie.

Emotions: Neutral

Thought 3: I never know what to say or do at parties. I'll make a fool of myself if I go.

Emotions: Anxious, sad

As you can see, the same event can lead to completely different emotions in different people. It all depends on our individual expectations, attitudes, and beliefs. For people with anxiety disorders, negative ways of thinking fuel the negative emotions of anxiety and fear. The goal of cognitive behavioral therapy for anxiety is to identify and correct these negative thoughts and beliefs. The idea is that if you change the way you think, you can change the way you feel.

Thought Challenging in CBT for Anxiety

Thought challenging—also known as cognitive restructuring—is a process in which you challenge the negative thinking patterns that contribute to your anxiety, replacing them with more positive, realistic thoughts. This involves three steps:

1. Identifying your negative thoughts. With anxiety disorders, situations are perceived as more dangerous than they really are. To someone with a germ phobia, for example, shaking another person's hand can seem life threatening. Although you may easily see that this is an irrational fear, identifying your own irrational, scary thoughts can be very difficult. One strategy is to ask yourself what you were thinking when you started feeling anxious. Your therapist will help you with this step.
2. Challenging your negative thoughts. In the second step, your therapist will teach you how to evaluate your anxiety-provoking thoughts. This involves questioning the evidence for your frightening thoughts, analyzing unhelpful beliefs, and testing out the reality of negative predictions. Strategies for challenging negative thoughts include conducting experiments,

weighing the pros and cons of worrying or avoiding the thing you fear, and determining the realistic chances that what you're anxious about will actually happen.

3. Replacing negative thoughts with realistic thoughts. Once you've identified the irrational predictions and negative distortions in your anxious thoughts, you can replace them with new thoughts that are more accurate and positive. Your therapist may also help you come up with realistic, calming statements you can say to yourself when you're facing or anticipating a situation that normally sends your anxiety levels soaring.

To understand how thought challenging works in cognitive behavioral therapy, consider the following example: Maria won't take the subway because she's afraid she'll pass out, and then everyone will think she's crazy. Her therapist has asked her to write down her negative thoughts, identify the errors—or cognitive distortions—in her thinking, and come up with a more rational interpretation. The results are below.

Challenging Negative Thoughts

Negative thought #1: What if I pass out on the subway?

Cognitive distortion: Predicting the worst

More realistic thought: I've never passed out before, so it's unlikely that I will on the subway.

Negative thought #2: If I pass out, it will be terrible.

Cognitive distortion: Blowing things out of proportion

More realistic thought: If I faint, I'll come to in a few moments. That's not so terrible.

Negative thought #3: People will think I'm crazy.

Cognitive distortion: conclusions

More realistic thought: People are more likely to be concerned if I'm okay.

Replacing negative thoughts with more realistic ones is easier said than done. Often, negative thoughts are part of a lifelong pattern of thinking. It takes practice to break the habit. That's why cognitive behavioral therapy includes practicing on your own at home as well. CBT may also include:

Learning to recognize when you're anxious and what that feels like in the body

Learning coping skills and relaxation techniques to counteract anxiety and panic

Confronting your fears (either in your imagination or in real life)

Exposure Therapy for Anxiety

Anxiety isn't a pleasant sensation, so it's only natural to avoid it if you can. One of the ways that people do this is by steering clear of the situations that make them anxious. If you have a fear of heights, you might drive three hours out of your way to avoid crossing a tall bridge. Or if the prospect of public speaking leaves your stomach in knots, you might skip your best friend's wedding in order to avoid giving a toast. Aside from the inconvenience factor, the problem with avoiding your fears is that you never have the chance to overcome them. In fact, avoiding your fears often makes them stronger.

Exposure therapy, as the name suggests, exposes you to the situations or objects you fear. The idea is that through repeated exposures, you'll feel an increasing sense of control over the situation and your anxiety will diminish. The exposure is done in one of two ways: Your therapist may ask you to imagine the scary situation, or you may confront it in real life. Exposure therapy may be used alone, or it may be conducted as part of cognitive behavioral therapy.

Systematic Desensitization

Rather than facing your biggest fear right away, which can be traumatizing, exposure therapy usually starts with a situation that's only mildly threatening and works up from there. This step-by-step approach is called systematic desensitization. Systematic desensitization allows you to gradually challenge your fears, build confidence, and master skills for controlling panic.

Facing a Fear of Flying

Step 1: Look at photos of planes.

Step 2: Watch a video of a plane in flight.

Step 3: Watch real planes take off.

Step 4: Book a plane ticket.

Step 5: Pack for your flight.

Step 6: Drive to the airport.

Step 7: Check in for your flight.

Step 8: Wait for boarding.

Step 9: Get on the plane.

Step 10: Take the flight.

Systematic desensitization involves three parts:

1. Learning relaxation skills. First, your therapist will teach you a relaxation technique, such as progressive muscle relaxation or deep breathing. You'll practice in therapy and on your own at home. Once you start confronting your fears, you'll use this relaxation technique to reduce your physical anxiety response (such as trembling and hyperventilating) and encourage relaxation.

2. Creating a step-by-step list. Next, you'll create a list of 10 to 20 scary situations that progress toward your final goal. For example, if your final goal is to overcome your fear of flying, you might start by looking at photos of planes and end with taking an actual flight. Each step should be as specific as possible, with a clear, measurable objective.

3. Working through the steps. Under the guidance of your therapist, you'll then begin to work through the list. The goal is to stay in each scary situation until your fears subside. That way, you'll learn that the feelings won't hurt you and they do go away. Every time the anxiety gets too intense, you will switch to the relaxation technique you learned. Once you're relaxed again, you can turn your attention back to the situation. In this way, you will work through the steps until you're able to complete each one without feeling overly distressed.

Complementary Therapies for Anxiety Disorders

As you explore your anxiety disorder in therapy, you may also want to experiment with complementary therapies designed to bring your overall stress levels down and help you achieve emotional balance.

Exercise is a natural stress buster and anxiety reliever. Research shows that as little as 30 minutes of exercise three to five times a week can provide significant anxiety relief. To achieve the maximum benefit, aim for at least an hour of aerobic exercise on most days.

Relaxation techniques such as mindfulness meditation and progressive muscle relaxation, when practiced regularly, can reduce anxiety and increase feelings of emotional well-being.

Biofeedback uses sensors that measure specific physiological functions—such as heart rate, breathing, and muscle tension—to teach you to recognize your body's anxiety response and learn how to control it using relaxation techniques.

Hypnosis is sometimes used in combination with CBT for anxiety. While you're in a state of deep relaxation, the hypnotherapist uses different therapeutic techniques to help you face your fears and look at them in new ways.

Making Anxiety Therapy Work for you

There is no quick fix for anxiety. Overcoming an anxiety disorder takes time and commitment. Therapy involves facing your fears rather than avoiding them, so sometimes you'll feel worse before you get better. The important thing is to stick with treatment and follow your therapist's advice. If you're feeling discouraged with the pace of recovery, remember that therapy for anxiety is very effective in the long run. You'll reap the benefits if you see it through.

You can also support your own anxiety therapy by making positive choices. Everything from your activity level to your social life affects anxiety. Set the stage for success by making a conscious decision to promote relaxation, vitality, and a positive mental outlook in your everyday life.

Learn about anxiety. In order to overcome anxiety, it's important to understand the problem. That's where education comes in. Education alone won't cure an anxiety disorder, but it will help you get the most out of therapy.

Cultivate your connections with other people. Loneliness and isolation set the stage for anxiety. Decrease your vulnerability by reaching out to others. Make it a point to see friends; join a self-help or support group; share your worries and concerns with a trusted loved one.

Adopt healthy lifestyle habits. Physical activity relieves tension and anxiety, so make time for regular exercise. Don't use alcohol and drugs to cope with your symptoms, and try to avoid stimulants such as caffeine and nicotine, which can make anxiety worse.

Reduce stress in your life. Examine your life for stress, and look for ways to minimize it. Avoid people who make you anxious, say no to extra responsibilities, and make time for fun and relaxation in your daily schedule.

How to Treat Delusional Disorder

Delusional disorders are characterized by a person not recognizing what is perceived and what is imagined. Often delusions include feelings of being followed, poisoned, or being conspired against. Other delusions can include believing you are famous or in power, or that a celebrity is in love with you. Generally, the experiences are either not true or very exaggerated. Delusional disorders can be treated with appropriate therapy, medication, and support.

Part 1. Readying yourself for Treatment

1. Treat safety concerns first. If the behaviors resulting from the delusions pose a threat to the self or to someone else, go immediately to the emergency department or call emergency services. Any dangerous actions (such as running into traffic, feeling suicidal, or stalking an individual) should be addressed first.

- Hospitalization may be necessary for treating risk factors.

2. Address violence or legal problems. Some people become violent or end up with legal charges as

a result of the delusions they experience. You may also become involved in the legal system for offenses such as stalking or harming someone you believe is following you. You may need to engage in programs aimed to decrease violence or other harmful behaviors.

- If you are arrested, cooperate. Seek any treatment suggested. You may want to request a psychological evaluation or participate in an addictions program as part of treatment.

3. Recognize the usefulness of treatment. Many people are unwilling to admit that the delusions pose a problem and are unwilling to seek help. If someone recommends treatment for you or points out how the delusions are affecting your life, listen up. It's okay to seek help and to admit that things are not going well. Treatment can help you build skills, engage constructively in social situations, and relieve stress associated with delusional disorder.

- Think about how you feel and how you relate to others. Have you noticed changes? Are you more paranoid, distrusting, or negative in your perception of people and things than you were before? Do you socially alienate yourself? Do you experience happiness and fulfillment every day.

Part 2. Working with a Therapist

1. Find a therapist you trust. Therapy is the most effective part of treatment for delusional disorder. The most important part of therapy is finding a therapist you trust. Because people with delusional disorder tend to be distrustful of others, establishing a solid relationship with a therapist

is a must. If you don't feel comfortable with your therapist, find a different one that helps you feel safe, trusting, and supported.

- Find a therapist who makes you feel unconditionally supported and not "crazy."
- Keep in mind that therapists and other mental health professionals take confidentiality very seriously. It is part of their professional code and they are also bound by federal and state laws to keep your information confidential. The only reason why a therapist might be required to report something that you said during a therapy session is if you are suicidal, someone else is at risk of being harmed, you or someone else is being abused, or the therapist has received a court order.

2. Engage in goal-oriented therapy. Make clear goals for therapy and daily living with your therapist. You may have your own goals (such as reducing distress), and the therapist may suggest goals such as improving social skills, engaging in positive behaviors, and improving personal, social, and occupational functioning.

- Find a therapist that will be direct and honest with you. Subtle cues may be less effective than direct comments.

3. Reduce distress. It can be helpful in therapy to work on reducing distress associated with the delusions. A therapist will listen and provide support. Your therapist may ask you questions regarding the state of your health: your sleeping patterns, eating habits, your ability to hold a job,

etc. If you are struggling in certain areas, the therapist will work to lower the distress the delusions cause. Work with your therapist, or practice these on your own to cope with distress:

- Deep breathing: Place your attention on your breath and slowly inhale and exhale. As you relax, feel the flow of each breath and the sensation of breath. Slowly lengthen your breath as you relax. You may choose to count the length of each inhale and exhale, lengthening each breath.
- Muscle relaxation: Release physical tension by systematically tensing and relaxing each muscle in your body. Start with your toes, feet, and legs, then move up to your pelvic area, stomach, chest, arms, neck, and face.
- Challenging negative thoughts: Recognize when you engage in catastrophizing (assuming the worst), personalization (taking blame), or "all or nothing" thoughts. Ask yourself, "Is this accurate? Making assumptions? Only seeing the negative? Are there any positive aspects to think about."

4. Start with small delusions. Once a therapist has established a good relationship with you and listens and understands your delusions, he or she will slowly begin to challenge the delusions. Your therapist will most likely challenge your smaller delusions first. Starting with the smaller, less-important delusions can help the therapist gauge the willingness to challenge the beliefs in therapy. If you are unwilling to give up the smaller delusions, it's likely therapy will be ongoing and long-term.

- The therapist will gently and gradually challenge the beliefs. This may include gentle questioning, such as, "You say a celebrity is in love with you. That must feel nice. When was the last time she visited you."

5. Continue attending therapy. It's not enough to go therapy a few times and say, "It didn't work."

Often, therapy will be long-term, so keep at it. Work at making life more productive without the presence of delusions.

- Remind yourself that you are working to improve your life and this can take time.

How to Treat Bipolar Disorder with Therapy

Psychotherapy, or "talk" therapy, is an important part of treatment for bipolar disorder. During therapy, you can discuss feelings, thoughts, and behaviors that cause you problems. Talk therapy can help you understand and hopefully master any problems that hurt your ability to function well in your life and career. It also helps you stay on your medication. It can help you maintain a positive self-image.

The types of psychotherapy used to treat bipolar disorder include:

- Behavioral therapy. This focuses on behaviors that decrease stress.
- Cognitive therapy. This type of approach involves learning to identify and modify the patterns of thinking that accompany mood shifts.
- Interpersonal therapy. This involves relationships and aims to reduce strains that the illness may place upon them.
- Social rhythm therapy. This helps you develop and maintain a normal sleep schedule and more predictable daily routines.

Support groups also help people with bipolar disorder. You receive encouragement, learn coping skills, and share concerns. You may feel less isolated as a result. Family members and friends may also benefit from a support group. They can gain a better understanding of the illness, share their concerns, and learn how to best support loved ones with bipolar disorder.

Education is another integral part of treatment for you and your family. People with bipolar disorder (and their families) often benefit from learning about the disorder - its symptoms, early signs of an episode, and types of treatment.

Also, taking these steps may help you cope with bipolar disorder:

- Establish routines. Regular sleep, eating, and activity appear to help people with bipolar disorder manage their moods.
- Identify symptoms. Even though the early warning signs of an approaching episode vary from person to person, together with a psychiatrist you can identify what behavior changes signal the onset of an episode for you. It may be needing less sleep to feel rested, buying things you can't afford or don't need, or becoming suddenly involved in religion or new activities and interests.
- Adapt. This can help you avoid embarrassing behavior during manic episodes and set realistic goals for treatment. Your doctor can help you prepare for possible future episodes

and manage fear about having more. A key part of adapting is to understand the types of stressors that might increase the risk for manic or depressive episodes and the lifestyle changes that can reduce them.

- Maintain a regular sleep pattern. Go to bed and wake up around the same times each day. Changes in sleep can disrupt the normal functioning of brain circuits involved in the processing of emotions, potentially triggering mood episodes.
- Do not use alcohol or street drugs. These substances can trigger or mimic mood episodes. They can also interfere with the effectiveness of medication.

How to Treat Co-Occurring Bipolar Disorder and Social Anxiety

Bipolar disorder is a mood condition that consists of intense highs and lows in temperament. It's called bipolar because it causes people to switch between two poles of mood, depression and mania. There are two types of bipolar disorder: Bipolar 1 and Bipolar 2. There is also something called Rapid Cycling Bipolar disorder, which causes a person to cycle quickly between mania and depression. A person suffering from this mental illness may experience the extreme sadness and hopelessness of depression for a period of time followed by high energy episodes of mania. If you have been diagnosed with bipolar disorder and social anxiety, it can be difficult to work out a treatment plan that addresses both conditions. It's important for you to work with a competent mental health provider who can monitor your symptoms and provide treatment. Learn how to treat co-occurring bipolar disorder and social anxiety by finding ways to cope with symptoms, working on your social confidence, and improving your relationships.

Part 1. Working with a Professional

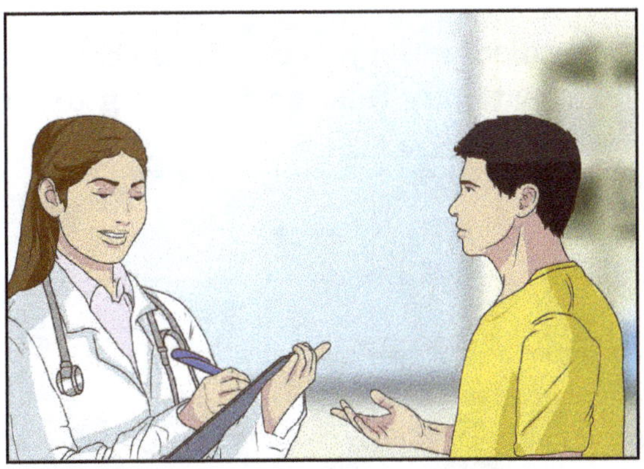

1. Get thorough evaluation to clarify your diagnosis. Because co-occurring bipolar disorder and social anxiety often worsen the course of bipolar symptoms, it's important that you have your condition evaluated by a mental health professional. Your doctor will want to identify which disorder came first, bipolar or anxiety? It is also significant to clarify the precise type of bipolar disorder affecting you as that can determine the treatment approach. There are three types:

- Bipolar I disorder involves the classic and severe symptoms of the disorder: one manic or mixed episode, and, usually one major depressive episode.
- Bipolar II involves similar features as Bipolar I, yet mania is a milder form known as hypomania. This type of bipolar has been found to be consistently related to social anxiety.
- Cyclothymia involves cycling mood swings of episodes of hypomania and mild depression, neither of which can be classified as full-blown mania or major depression.

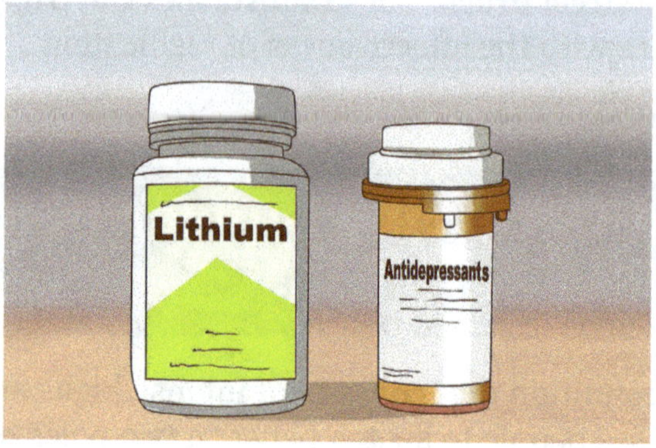

2. Decide on a medication regimen that helps with both disorders. Bipolar disorder and social anxiety are particularly challenging to treat using pharmacological approaches because the traditional treatment options for each singular condition poses problems when they are treated concurrently.

- Lithium is commonly prescribed for bipolar disorder. However, you cannot take this medication if you are pregnant, due to the risk of birth defects.
- For instance, antidepressants are a typical course of treatment for anxiety disorder, but these medications are known to induce mania in bipolar patients. Benzodiazepines are effective at treating anxiety and bipolar disorder, but they are associated with physiological dependency. If you are concerned about addiction, then long acting benzodiazepines, such as Klonopin, might be a good alternative.
- One type of medications called antipsychotics have shown effectiveness in the treatment of social phobia in bipolar patients. Talk to your doctor to see if this type of medication is appropriate for your case.

3. Receive behavior therapy. Relaxation training and cognitive behavioral therapy, which are

commonly prescribed in the treatment of anxiety disorders, may be useful for people with bipolar disorder, too. Psychotherapy may involve working with a therapist to develop coping mechanisms, learning emotional regulation, repairing problematic relationships, and overcoming negative thought patterns.

- Ask your doctor for a referral to a mental health therapist who has experience treating both social anxiety and bipolar disorder. Consult with a few therapists to determine which one you feel most comfortable with and to decide if their therapeutic style aligns with your needs.

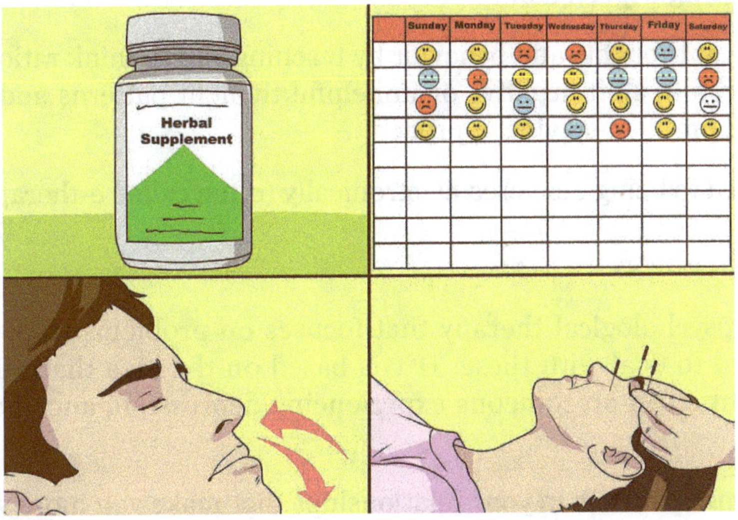

4. Try alternative treatment approaches. There are a range of complementary treatments that some people may use in the management of bipolar and social anxiety symptoms. It's important to discuss any new therapies with your doctor and mental health provider to be sure that they will not interact with your current treatment plan.

- Alternative treatments for bipolar and social anxiety may include natural and herbal supplements, mood charting, mindfulness, deep breathing techniques, and acupuncture.

How to Treat Depression with Therapy

Psychological Treatments for Depression

Psychological treatments (also known as talking therapies) can help you change your thinking patterns and improve your coping skills so you're better equipped to deal with life's stresses and conflicts. As well as supporting your recovery, psychological therapies can also help you stay well by identifying and changing unhelpful thoughts and behavior.

There are several types of effective psychological treatments for depression, as well as different delivery options. Some people prefer to work one on one with a professional, while others get more out of a group environment. A growing number of online programs, or e-therapies, are also available.

Cognitive Behavior Therapy

CBT is a structured psychological treatment which recognises that the way we think (cognition) and act (behavior) affects the way we feel. CBT is one of the most effective treatments for depression, and has been found to be useful for a wide range of ages, including children, adolescents, adults and older people.

CBT involves working with a professional (therapist) to identify thought and behavior patterns that are either making you more likely to become depressed, or stopping you from getting better when you're experiencing depression.

It works to change your thoughts and behavior by teaching you to think rationally about common difficulties, helping you to shift negative or unhelpful thought patterns and reactions to a more realistic, positive and problem-solving approach.

CBT is also well-suited to being delivered electronically (often called e-therapies).

Interpersonal Therapy

IPT is a structured psychological therapy that focuses on problems in personal relationships and the skills needed to deal with these. IPT is based on the idea that relationship problems can have a significant effect on someone experiencing depression, and can even contribute to the cause.

IPT helps you recognise patterns in your relationships that make you more vulnerable to depression. Identifying these patterns means you can focus on improving relationships, coping with grief and finding new ways to get along with others.

Behavior Therapy

While behavior therapy is a major component of cognitive behavior therapy (CBT), unlike CBT it doesn't attempt to change beliefs and attitudes. Instead it focuses on encouraging activities that are rewarding, pleasant or satisfying, aiming to reverse the patterns of avoidance, withdrawal and inactivity that make depression worse.

Mindfulness-based Cognitive Therapy

MBCT is generally delivered in groups and involves a type of meditation called 'mindfulness meditation'. This teaches you to focus on the present moment – just noticing whatever you're experiencing, whether it's pleasant or unpleasant – without trying to change it. At first, this approach is used to focus on physical sensations (like breathing), but then moves on to feelings and thoughts.

MBCT can help to stop your mind wandering off into thoughts about the future or the past, and avoid unpleasant thoughts and feelings. This is thought to be helpful in preventing depression from returning because it encourages you to notice feelings of sadness and negative thinking patterns early on, before they become fixed. As a result, you're able to deal with warning signs earlier and more effectively.

How to Treat Obsessive-Compulsive Disorder

Clinical and animal research sponsored by NIMH and other scientific organizations has provided information leading to both pharmacological and behavioral treatments that can benefit the person with OCD. While some benefit significantly from behavior therapy and others are helped by pharmacotherapy, research indicates that a robust treatment of OCD includes both medication and therapy. Patients may begin with medication to gain control over their symptoms and then continue with behavior therapy. Which therapy to use should be decided by the individual patient in consultation with his or her therapist.

Medication

Clinical trials in recent years have shown that drugs that affect the neurotransmitter serotonin can significantly decrease the symptoms of OCD. The first of these serotonin re-uptake inhibitors (SRIs) specifically approved for the use in the treatment of OCD was the tricyclic antidepressant clomipramine (Anafranil). It was followed by "selective" serotonin re-uptake inhibitors (SSRIs). Those that have been approved by the Food and Drug Administration for the treatment of OCD are citalopram (Celexa), flouxetine (Prozac), fluvoxamine (Luvox), paroxetine (Paxil), and sertraline (Zoloft).

Large studies have shown that more than three-quarters of patients are helped by these medications at least a little. And in more than half of patients, medications relieve symptoms of OCD by diminishing the frequency and intensity of the obsessions and compulsions. Improvement usually takes at least three weeks or longer. If a patient does not respond well to one of these medications, or has unacceptable side effects, another SRI may give a better response. For patients who are only partially responsive to these medications, research is being conducted on the use of an SRI as the primary medication and one of a variety of medications as an additional drug (an augmenter). Medications are of help in controlling the symptoms of OCD, but often, if the medication is discontinued, relapse will follow.

Behavior Therapy

Cognitive behavior therapy (CBT) has been shown to be the most effective type of psychotherapy for this disorder. CBT aims to diminish thoughts and beliefs in order to help modify behaviors and vice versa. Medication and CBT together are considered to be better than either treatment alone at reducing symptoms.

A specific behavior therapy approach called "exposure and response prevention" is effective for many people with OCD. In this approach, the patient deliberately and voluntarily confronts the feared object or idea, either directly or by imagination. At the same time, the therapist, and possibly others the patient has recruited for assistance, offer support and structure, strongly encouraging the patient to refrain from using rituals or avoidance. For example, a compulsive hand washer may be encouraged to touch an object believed to be contaminated and then urged to avoid washing for several hours, until the anxiety provoked has greatly decreased. Treatment then proceeds on a step-by-step basis, guided by the patient's ability to tolerate the anxiety and control the rituals. As treatment progresses, most patients gradually experience less anxiety from the obsessive thoughts and are able to resist the compulsive urges.

Other forms of therapy can also provide effective ways of reducing stress or anxiety by helping the patient become aware of and resolve inner conflicts.

Ways to Make Treatment More Effective

Many people with anxiety disorders benefit from joining a self-help or support group and sharing their problems and achievements with others. Internet chat rooms can also be useful in this regard, but any advice received over the Internet should be used with caution as Internet acquaintances have usually never seen each other and false identities are common. Talking with a trusted friend or member of the clergy can also provide support but is not a substitute for care from a mental health professional.

Stress management techniques and meditation can help people with anxiety disorders calm themselves and may enhance the effects of therapy. There is preliminary evidence that aerobic exercise may have a calming effect. Since caffeine, certain illicit drugs, and even some over-the-counter cold medications can aggravate the symptoms of anxiety disorders, they should be avoided. Check with your physician or pharmacist before taking any additional medications.

The family is very important in the recovery of a person with an anxiety disorder. Ideally, the family should be supportive and avoid perpetuating their loved one's symptoms. Relatives should not trivialize the disorder or demand improvement without treatment. When a family member suffers from obsessive-compulsive disorder, it's helpful to be patient about any progress and acknowledge successes, no matter how small.

How to Treat Psychotic Depression

Psychotic depression is a sub-type of major depressive disorder, characterized by the presence of psychotic features. Psychotic depression may involve hallucinations and delusions. This condition can interfere with regular activities and requires immediate attention. To effectively manage psychotic depression, be aware of symptoms and treatment options.

Method 1. Considering Treatment

1. Identify the symptoms. Being aware of common symptoms will help you and your loved ones

treat your condition and alleviate some of your difficulties. Some of the symptoms and conditions associated with psychotic depression are:

- Sleep disturbance.
- Decreased appetite.
- Suicidal ideation.
- Agitation and anger.
- Hallucination and delusions.
- Irritability.
- Deteriorating social and occupational life.

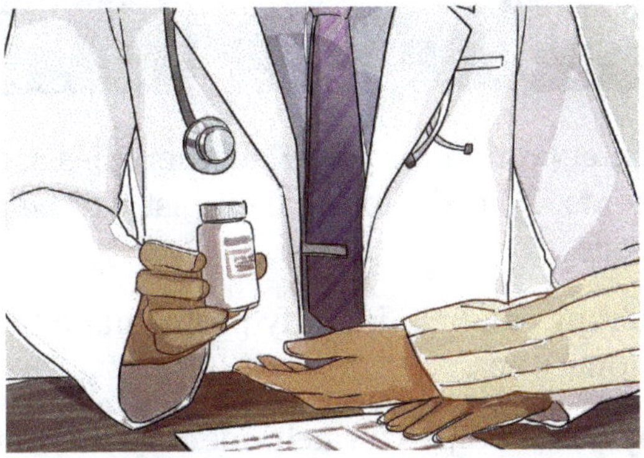

2. Seek medical treatment and adhere to it. Medication is commonly necessary to treat a person with psychotic depression. A doctor may prescribe an antidepressant to treat symptoms generally associated with depression and an antipsychotic to treat the symptoms of psychosis. Antipsychotics may only be prescribed for a short time. Depression will likely be the main focus of treatment.

- Always comply with treatment guidelines and follow the directions of your psychiatrist, as well as your psychologist.
- Make sure you do not stop taking your medication without consulting your doctor. Suddenly stopping medication may be dangerous and may result in relapse.

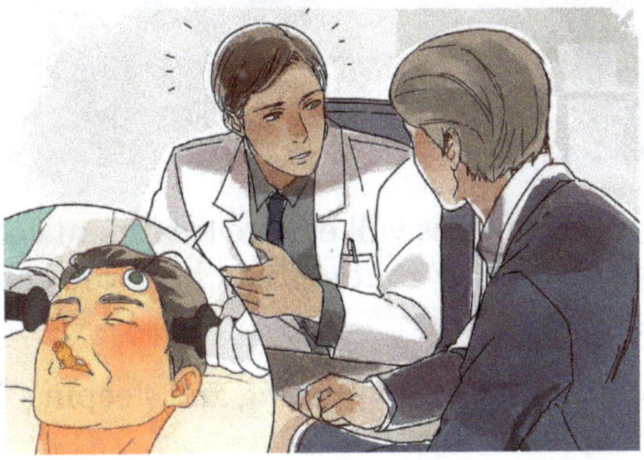

3. Discuss electroconvulsive therapy (ECT) with your doctor. Psychotic depression is one of few disorders that may be treated by ECT. The treatment involves passing electrical currents through

the brain, triggering brief seizures that change brain chemistry.

- While current ECT practices are relatively safe, be sure to discuss possible side effects with your doctor.

4. Find the best therapeutic intervention for you. Talk therapies are often recommended in conjunction with medical treatments. Your doctor or therapist will be able to help you find the best treatment options for your needs.

- Cognitive behavior therapy can help identify problematic thoughts and behaviors and replace them with functional ones.
- Rational emotive behavior therapy can help identify the unnecessary demands from the self, the world and others, and contributes to change by challenge irrational ideas associated with depressive rumination.

5. Develop daily routines. Regular routines will ensure treatment compliance and shift your focus to functional activities. Following regular routines can help you relieve depressive symptoms by adding structure to your days.

- Schedule your day, including grooming, eating and sleeping, in addition to typically scheduled items like work or appointments.
- Include healthy activities, like exercise, and pleasurable activities, like hobbies.

Method 2. Finding Support

1. Participate in or organize a support group. As a person having depressive or suicidal thoughts, potentially suffering from hallucinations and delusions, you should build up a strong network of social support. As the psychotic features become less severe, having a network that can help counsel you and identify your misconceptions, delusions, and hallucinations is very helpful.

- Look for support groups at local community centers. If you are unable to participate in groups in your community, look for online support groups.

2. Involve trusted family members. Invite family members to participate in support groups with you or to accompany you to a counseling appointment. This will help them better understand your experiences and feel more comfortable talking to you about your condition.

- Family therapy is a great way to involve multiple family members with the guidance of a mental health professional.

3. Become an advocate. Join a local advocacy group for depression or psychosis to help you better

understand your condition and effectively communicate with others. This will create networking opportunities and help you identify resources.

- National Alliance on Mental Illness is a good place to start.

Method 3. Preventing Relapse

1. Eliminate negative beliefs. Feelings of worthlessness, hopelessness and helplessness are common in people with depression. These feelings can be further exacerbated by psychotic features such as delusions, which may have paranoid, persecutory or somatic themes. Challenge negative beliefs frequently to reduce negative self-talk.

- Identify negative thoughts by recognizing key words. If your thoughts involve words like "can't", "never", and "won't", they are probably negative.
- Consider alternative possibilities. When you catch yourself thinking negatively, try stating the thought with positive terms, like can and will.

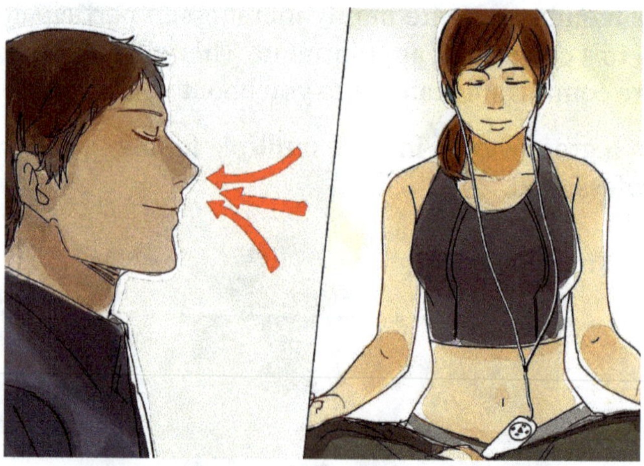

2. Manage stress to reduce symptoms of depression and prevent relapse. Stress contributes to depression and may trigger relapse. Healthy coping strategies will help mitigate the effects of stress.

- Exercise promotes a sense of wellbeing and contributes to resilience.

- Practice deep breathing or relaxation exercises.
- Schedule regular dates with friends and family to maintain healthy relationships.

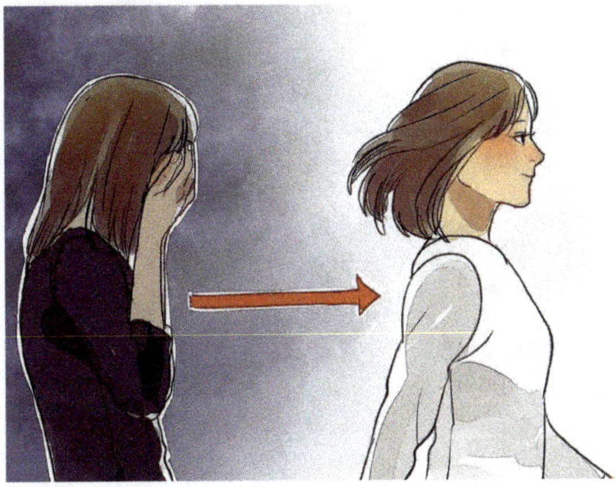

3. Remain hopeful. You are not the only person to experience this. Psychotic depression can be effectively treated and recovery is likely.

- Keep track of your progress to maintain motivation.

How to Treat Schizophrenia

Schizophrenia is a psychiatric disorder that may make you feel like you have lost touch with reality. Although schizophrenia is considered a chronic mental illness, it is treatable. In fact, many people with schizophrenia lead positive and productive lives with jobs, passions, and healthy relationships. Schizophrenia is best treated by an experienced mental health provider. See a doctor, get needed support, and implement positive lifestyle habits to manage schizophrenia.

Method 1. Seeking Professional Help

1. See a doctor for a thorough diagnosis. To receive an adequate diagnosis of schizophrenia, start by visiting your family physician. This doctor may be your first line of treatment for schizophrenia.

They can conduct a physical examination, review your medical history, and help rule out other conditions that may cause similar symptoms.

2. Undergo testing. If your doctor doesn't find any medical explanation for your symptoms, they may refer you to a mental health provider for further testing. A psychiatrist or psychologist may perform a battery of tests to check your mental status and ask questions about your symptoms.

- Be honest and upfront about any symptoms you experience. Giving your mental health provider the full picture of your symptoms ensures that you receive the right diagnosis.
- Your doctor may ask whether you have seen or felt things that others didn't (hallucinations) or have unshakable beliefs that aren't based in reality (delusions).

3. Discuss medication options with your doctor. Medication is typically at the foundation of treatment for schizophrenia. These medications work by improving the balance of chemicals in the brain that make you lose touch with reality. Talk to your doctor to determine which medication is right for you.

- The most effective medications for schizophrenia include antipsychotics, particularly second-generation medications that have fewer serious side effects (also known as atypical antipsychotics). Keep in mind, however, that you may have to try several medications before finding the one that best helps you manage your schizophrenia symptoms.
- Follow your doctor's orders when taking your medications. Never stop taking your meds unless your doctor has instructed you to, as doing so could lead to serious side effects.

- If you experience negative side effects from your medication, let your doctor know as soon as possible. They will likely be able to switch you to a different medication.

4. Consider psychotherapy. Although medication is the best way to reduce schizophrenia symptoms, many people also find that talk therapy also helps them manage schizophrenia. Psychotherapy may involve educating yourself about how schizophrenia impacts your functioning, helping you cope with stress that exacerbates symptoms, and conducting reality testing.

- In addition to one-on-one therapy, you might also consider group therapy or family therapy. Both of which can help you learn to better manage living with schizophrenia.

5. Ask about electroconvulsive therapy. Electroconvulsive therapy, or ECT, is a procedure in which currents are sent through the brain to reverse the symptoms of severe mental illness. When used in combination with medication, ECT has proven to be an effective form of treating severe forms of schizophrenia that are resistant to typical treatments.

- If you are failing to see improvements from second-generation antipsychotics, you might ask your doctor about ECT.

Method 2. Getting Support for Schizophrenia

1. Connect with a community intervention team. After you are diagnosed with schizophrenia, your health care providers should set you up with a community mental health team, sometimes called assertive community treatment (ACT). These teams consist of highly experienced professionals from a variety of backgrounds who can provide day-to-day individualized treatment and support for living with schizophrenia.

- Your team might consist of psychiatrists, psychologists, mental health nurses, pharmacists, counselors, social workers, and occupational therapists.

2. Involve your friends and family. Receiving support from your loved ones is critical to your ability to manage schizophrenia. Include your family and friends in doctor visits, ACT team meetings, therapy sessions, and support groups. Encourage them to ask your treatment team any questions they need to better support you.

- You might also make special requests as to how your loved ones can support you. These may include helping you spot early warning signs, helping you remember your medications, accompanying you to appointments, and helping you relearn skills to function in everyday life.

3. Participate in a support group. Being diagnosed with schizophrenia can make you feel isolated and misunderstood. That's why it's a great idea to connect with other people who are living with the condition. Self-help and support groups are designed to help you build relationships with others with schizophrenia.

- In support groups, you might discuss helpful coping strategies, get education about managing schizophrenia, and share stories about what's it like living with the disorder.
- Ask your doctor or therapist about schizophrenia support groups in your area.

4. Get social skills training. Ask your community mental health team or support group about how you can receive social skills training. These behavioral interventions can help you better function in the community and feel more capable of managing schizophrenia.

- Social skills training can improve your quality of life by helping you behave appropriately in social situations, solve problems, communicate more effectively with those around you, and deal with everyday life stress.

5. Receive vocational rehabilitation. Doing meaningful work in your community can also help

improve your quality of life with schizophrenia. Consider getting vocational training to help you develop transferrable skills, look for a job that suits your lifestyle and condition, and learn how to manage your money.

- In some cases, vocational training may be grouped in with social skills training.

How to Diagnose a Brief Psychotic Disorder

Sometimes symptoms of a psychotic disorder can come on suddenly and result from a stressful event. It can be scary to see yourself or someone you love go through a brief psychotic disorder, but getting proper help can make things easier. To receive a proper diagnosis, make an appointment with a psychologist or therapist. However, you can also check for symptoms, consider any recent stressors, and try to rule out other potential causes of your symptoms.

Part 1. Checking for Symptoms

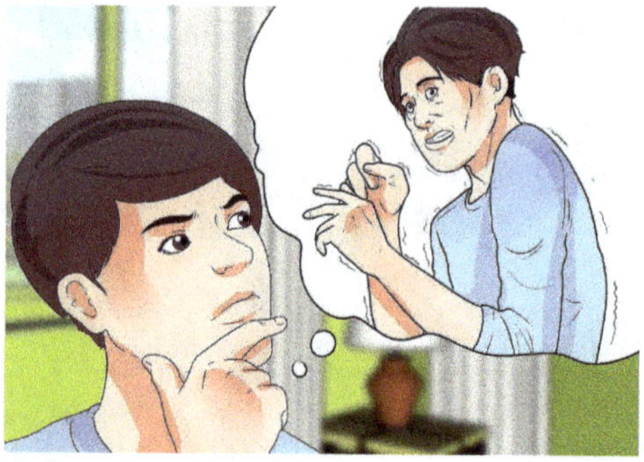

1. Notice the presence of delusions. Delusions refer to strange ideas or beliefs that a person expresses. They are often unrealistic and illogical. Other people may find the ideas or beliefs to be strange and unbelievable.

- Types of delusions can include thinking that something that something is happening when it is not really happening, such as that your significant other is cheating on you when he or she is not. Delusions can also be more bizarre, such as believing that someone has taken out all of your internal organs and replaced them with robotic parts without leaving any scars.

2. Acknowledge hallucinations. Hallucinations refer to experiencing things that other people do

not experience. This can include hearing voices or seeing things that others do not see. Some examples of hallucinations include feeling sensations in or on the body, such as something crawling or movement in the internal organs. A person may also hear sounds such as footsteps, voices, or music. If hearing voices, they may be critical, positive, or neutral.

- Sometimes people report hearing voices that command them to hurt people. If you hear voices telling you to hurt yourself or someone else, seek help immediately.

3. Recognize disorganized behavior. Disorganized behavior can include strange or out-of-character actions. This can include agitated or excessive movement, strange or bizarre posturing, repetitive behaviors, or a complete lack of movement. This type of behavior differs greatly from normal behavior.

4. Notice changes in speech patterns. Changes may occur in speech or language. These changes can include incoherence or derailment. With incoherence, it may be hard to understand what the person is talking about. With derailment, the person might jump from one idea to the next, such as saying, "I found an abandoned house in the woods. I saw my sister in the mall."

- The content of the speech may also be irrational or nonsensical, and it may be difficult to keep up. This type of speech makes it difficult to communicate.

5. Notice sudden onset. Along with being brief, this psychotic disorder may come on suddenly. The experience of extreme stress can cause a quick onset of symptoms and decrease in functioning. Some examples of the types of extreme stress that may bring on a brief psychotic disorder include:

- Losing a loved one.
- Suffering from a traumatic event, such as a car crash or physical attack.
- Losing one's job.
- A family conflict, such as getting a divorce or ending a long term relationship.
- Severe illness.

Part 2. Examining Recent Stressors

1. Notice the presence of a major stressor. Brief psychotic episodes result from a traumatic event or stressor that occurs. This can include the death of a loved one or another major life-altering event. It can also occur during pregnancy or within four weeks of childbirth.

- If you or a loved one may be experiencing a brief psychotic episode, ask yourself what may have triggered the episode. What events happened beforehand that may have contributed stress?

2. Recognize who is most commonly affected. Brief psychotic episodes are most commonly diagnosed in people in their 20's, 30's, and 40's. If a person has been diagnosed with a personality disorder, this may increase the chance of having a brief psychosis.

3. Note the duration of symptoms. Typically, symptoms last for one to 30 days. People generally make a full recovery after the episode. If symptoms persist over 30 days, additional treatment may be needed. You may also want to consider medication or further services.

4. Look out for suicidal thoughts. One risk factor to look out for regarding brief psychotic disorder

is an increase in suicidal thoughts or behaviors. Be especially aware of this risk if there is a past history of suicidal thoughts, a family history of suicide, or previous suicide attempts.

- If you are concerned, keep lethal weapons and other means away, such as knives, pills, or guns. Also, avoid alcohol and other substances that may alter one's ability to make decisions.
- If symptoms are violent or threatening in any way, seek immediate help. Go to the emergency department or call emergency services.

Part 3. Ruling out other Causes

1. Take note of any presence of drugs, alcohol or other substances. The episode is not considered a brief psychotic disorder if the person has taken any drugs or substances recently. The symptoms cannot be a direct result of drugs, alcohol, or any substances.

- If the person has taken substances, it's important to discuss when the substance was taken, how much was taken, and when symptoms began to occur.

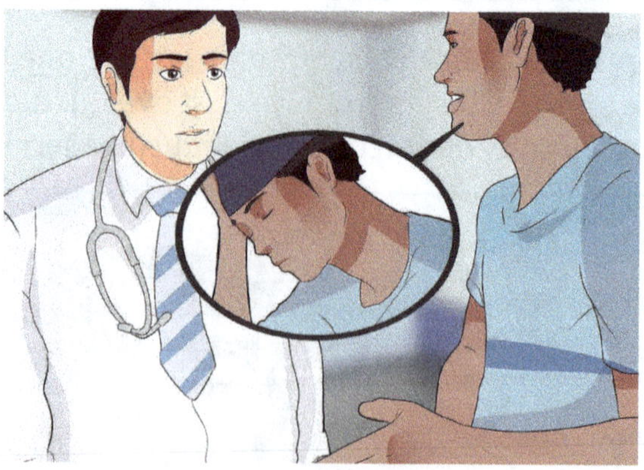

2. Ask whether symptoms are related to a mood disorder. Both depression and bipolar disorder can involve psychotic symptoms. If ruling out depression or bipolar disorder, it's important to examine previous mental health problems with depression and to also learn about any family history of depression or bipolar disorder.

- Delusions associated with depression also differ. For example, a person may express delusions consistent with mood, such as feeling dead. Bipolar delusions often present as over the top, such as believing you are invincible, have special abilities (like flying), or believe yourself to be a highly spiritual figure or God.

3. Examine enduring symptoms. If symptoms persist beyond one month, a psychologist or psychiatrist may diagnose the person with schizophrenia or schizoaffective disorder. These disorders include chronic symptoms of psychosis. Monitor symptoms and see if they improve. If not, a form of schizophrenia may be responsible for the symptoms.

- To properly treat schizophrenia, a combination of therapy and medication is best. Seek mental health treatment as soon as possible to decrease the likelihood of worsening symptoms.

How to Recognize and Treat Postpartum Psychosis

Compared to the "baby blues" and postpartum depression, postpartum psychosis is not as rare as it is told to be, affecting only about 10-15% of women who give birth. The condition is, however, very serious, and it can be dangerous to mothers, babies and even fathers, seeing men can get postpartum depression too. Because women with postpartum psychosis lose their connection with reality, suicide and violence may become possibilities. Recognizing the signs as quickly as possible is important for early and effective treatment. If you think that you (or someone you love) may have postpartum psychosis, start with Step 1 to learn more.

Part 1. Recognizing the Symptoms of Postpartum Psychosis

1. Watch for hallucinations. Women who develop postpartum psychosis often see or hear things

that are not really there. These hallucinations may be frightening, upsetting, or disorienting. They may come and go, or they may persist. Hallucinations are one of the major signs that distinguishes postpartum psychosis from postpartum depression, and it requires immediate medical intervention.

2. Take confusion seriously. Confusion also distinguishes postpartum psychosis from postpartum depression. Even healthy new mothers may seem exhausted and mentally foggy, but these symptoms should not evolve into true confusion or bewilderment. A woman with postpartum psychosis may seem puzzled by what's going on around her unable to understand what others are saying to her.

3. Look for delusions. Along with hallucinations and confusion, delusions – strange but strongly held beliefs that a rational person would know to be false – are one of the chief symptoms that distinguishes postpartum psychosis from postpartum depression. Delusions also require immediate medical treatment. They may not cause a woman to hurt herself or someone else, but in some cases, they do lead to violence.

- These delusions, perhaps in combination with hallucinations, may make a woman paranoid or suspicious. Someone with postpartum psychosis may think her friends and family members are lying to her or trying to hurt her; she may feel that she is being watched or followed.

4. Pay attention to mood swings. Mood swings are a common symptom for women with postpartum depression and anxiety, and they also play a role in postpartum psychosis. Women who develop postpartum psychosis tend to move quickly from one emotional state to another; they may suddenly find themselves overwhelmingly sad, distressed, irritated, or angry, and they may or may not be able to pinpoint any reason for the abrupt shift in mood.

5. Monitor sleep patterns. Difficulty sleeping is also characteristic of all the postpartum psychiatric conditions, but it may be especially pronounced in women with postpartum psychosis. They may develop persistent insomnia, or they may feel that they do not need to sleep at all.

- This symptom can be especially difficult to detect because most new mothers, even perfectly healthy ones, struggle with sleep. Newborns do not sleep reliably, and they must eat frequently, which can disrupt their mothers' sleeping patterns. For women with postpartum psychosis, though, difficulties with sleep persist even when they are given the opportunity to rest (as when a spouse, partner, friend, or relative agrees to care for the baby temporarily).

6. Note any hyperactivity. Postpartum psychosis can make a woman seem manic, agitated, or unusually energetic. She may not be able to sit still or calm down.

7. Take feelings of "craziness" seriously. Women with postpartum psychosis sometimes articulate the sense that they are "going crazy" or "losing their minds." Do not dismiss these feelings; get help.

8. Be especially vigilant during the first few weeks after delivery. Technically, postpartum psychosis can develop at up to six months postpartum, but almost all cases occur during the first four weeks. If you are a new mother yourself, or if your wife or partner recently gave birth, pay particular attention to mental and psychological symptoms during this early period.

9. Consider risk factors. Women with a history of bipolar disorder have a much higher incidence

of postpartum psychosis, as do women who have had postpartum psychosis before. Family history may also play a role: if a new mother has a family history of mental illness, her risk of developing postpartum psychosis increases. Be particularly vigilant in these cases.

- Note, however, that half of all women who develop postpartum psychosis have none of these risk factors. The disorder sometimes occurs for no discernible reason at all.

Part 2. Diagnosing Postpartum Psychosis

1. Get medical help immediately. If you think you may have postpartum psychosis, see your doctor or go to an emergency room or urgent care center right away. If someone close to you is showing signs of postpartum psychosis, do everything in your power to get that person treatment – she may be too disoriented or unstable to recognize that she needs help on her own.

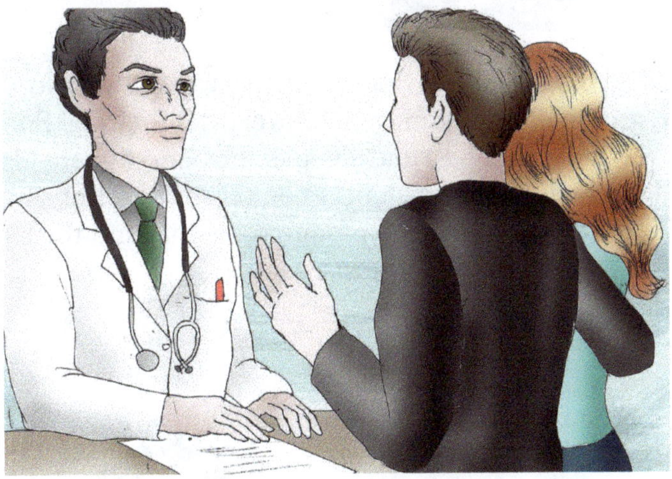

2. Provide as much information as possible. The doctor should ask for a complete medical history and a detailed description of any symptoms. Provide as much information as you can, and be honest – do not attempt to conceal the severity of your symptoms or act like you are okay when you are not.

- If the person getting evaluated for postpartum psychosis is not you but rather your wife, partner, or friend, you may need to provide some or all of this information yourself. She may not be in a position to speak rationally or to give a detailed account of her symptoms.

3. Rule out potential medical causes. Some of the symptoms of postpartum psychosis can occasionally be caused by underlying medical conditions: a serious infection, a very high fever, or a neurological problem, for example. A doctor should evaluate symptoms and perform tests, usually including basic blood work, to rule out potential medical issues.

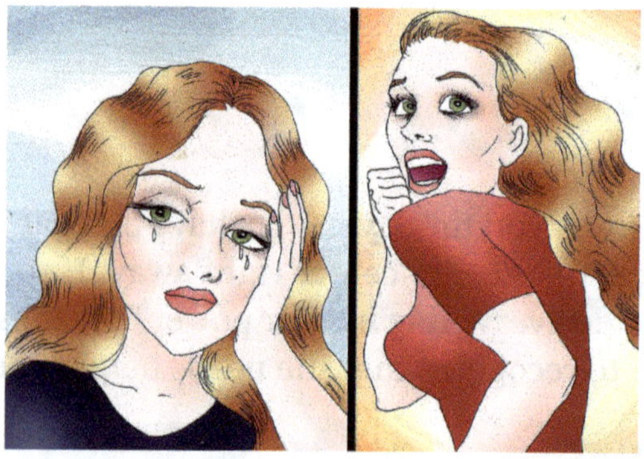

4. Distinguish between depression and psychosis. Many women develop postpartum depression after the birth of a baby, and their symptoms can be very debilitating. Some of these symptoms – especially mood swings, extreme sadness, and sleep disturbances – are also indicative of postpartum psychosis. A good doctor will distinguish between these conditions by looking for evidence of psychotic episodes: hallucinations, delusions, paranoia, mania, and the like.

5. Get a specific diagnosis. Knowing exactly what's going on is the first step to treating the condition and recovering completely. If the doctor rules out underlying medical causes and notes a

psychotic component to the mental disturbance, he or she may diagnose you (or your wife or partner) with postpartum psychosis.

Part 3. Treating Postpartum Psychosis

1. Follow your doctor's instructions. A woman with postpartum psychosis may insist that she needs to be at home, caring for her baby, but this condition requires that you follow medical advice. Doing otherwise poses a threat to both mother and baby.

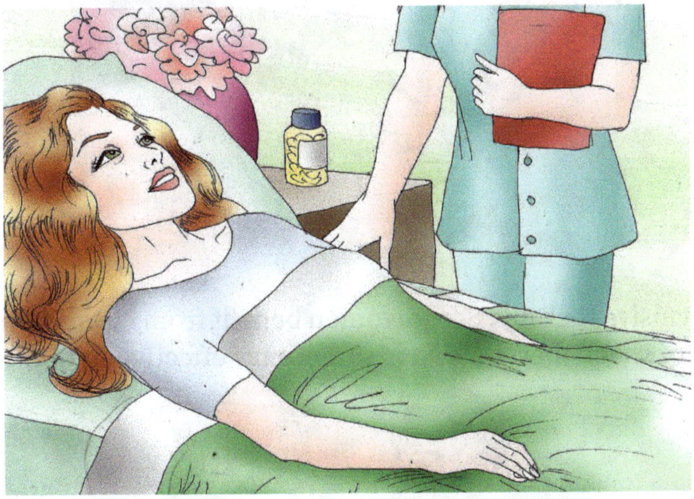

2. Understand that hospitalization is often required. Many women with postpartum psychosis need to be hospitalized so that medical staff can monitor them until they stabilize. Entering a hospital – especially a psychiatric hospital, as frequently necessary – can be upsetting, especially for new mothers, who may insist that they need to be at home. But this step is often necessary for effective treatment.

- If your wife, partner, or loved one must be hospitalized with postpartum psychosis, try to assure her that hospitalization is temporary and that full-time, effective treatment will help her get home to her baby as quickly as possible. Do everything in your power to convince her that she is doing the right thing for herself and for her newborn.

3. Take recommended medications. Women with postpartum psychosis are typically prescribed some combination of antipsychotic drugs and mood stabilizers. When taken as directed, these drugs are generally quite effective.

- These drugs may or may not be safe to take when breastfeeding, so talk to your doctor and weigh the risks and benefits of particular medications. Remember that treating the postpartum psychosis should be the primary concern, followed by continuation of breastfeeding.

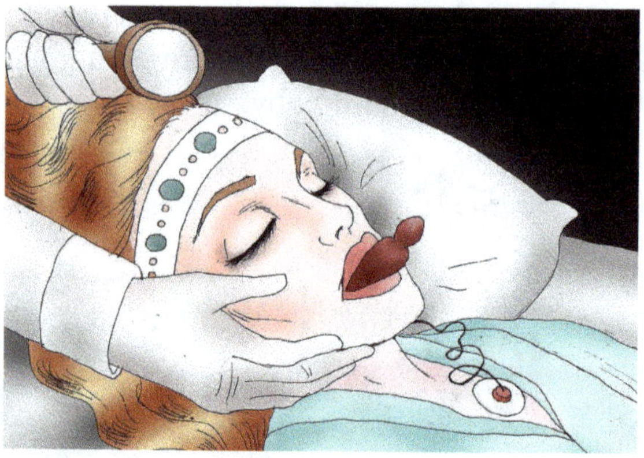

4. Consider electroconvulsive therapy. Some women benefit from electroconvulsive therapy (ECT). This is a modern form of shock therapy that is sometimes effective in treating psychotic episodes.

5. Add counseling. Postpartum psychosis is a medical condition, and it demands medical treatment. In addition, though, talk therapy may be beneficial, especially the disorder begins to recede.

A counselor can help you (or your wife, partner, or loved one) deal with the symptoms of postpartum psychosis and the trauma that the condition can inflict. Moving forward, a counselor can also help you deal with any feelings of doubt or guilt about motherhood, which many women experience after postpartum depression, anxiety, or psychosis.

- If you are not sure you absolutely need counseling or cannot afford, talking it out with your significant other or family member is amazing therapy in its own. Spending an hour or two on its own can make a difference and can relieve you of some symptoms.

CHAPTER

4

Improving Mental Health

Certain practices and lifestyle choices can ensure mental health for all individuals. Activities such as sports, cycling and athletics, meditation, recreation and occupational therapies, walks, crafts making, music therapy, dance therapy, art therapy, etc. can promote healing and rejuvenation on a psychological level. This chapter closely examines the techniques of improving mental health by targeting specific aspects of memory, mental strength, mental stamina, brain age and nourishment, for a holistic understanding of mental health.

How to Improve your Memory

There is no such thing as a "bad memory", and anyone can improve their memory, as long as you are not suffering from memory loss as a medical condition. If you want to improve your memory, there are a number of things you can do, from eating blueberries to using a variety of mnemonic devices. If you're optimistic and dedicated, you'll be able to improve your memory, whether you want to win the World Memory Championships, ace your history test, or simply remember where you put your keys.

Part 1. Using Mnemonic Devices

1. Use association to remember facts. To use association effectively, you can create an image in your mind to help you remember a word or an image. For example, if you have a hard time remembering that JFK was the president involved in the Bay of Pigs invasion, just picture the handsome president swimming in an ocean surrounded by happy, oinking pigs. This is absolutely silly, but this concrete image in your mind will forever help you link the president with this event.

- By creating a visual, your brain can fixate on a single, easy-to-identify piece of information. When you recall that single symbol, you can also recall the larger strand of information you assigned to it. For example, as you place your car keys in your purse, imagine your purse suddenly growing wheels and speeding away. Since the image is such a strange one, you're more likely to remember it later, which will also help you remember that your car keys are inside it.

- The more unique or unusual the image is, the easier it will be for your brain to remember it.

2. Use association to remember numbers. Let's say you keep forgetting your student ID every time you need to use it again. Just break down the number into smaller chunks and create images associated with those chunks. Let's say the number is 12-7575-23. Find a way to make these numbers meaningful. Let's say "12" happens to be your house number, "75" happens to be your grandmother's age, and the number "23" is Michael Jordan's jersey number. Here's what you can visualize to remember the number:

    - Picture your house with two copies of your grandmother standing to the right, showing that the house comes first. Then imagine Michael Jordan standing to the right of your grandmothers. There you have it - 12 (your house), 7575 (double-dose of Grandma) and 23, the basketball star.

3. Use chunking. Chunking is a way of grouping things together to help you memorize them. Random lists of things (a shopping list, for example) can be especially difficult to remember. To make it easier, try categorizing the individual things from the list. For example, list all of the fruits together, the dairy products together, and the bread products together. Alternatively, you can chunk your list by the starting letter of each item; you need to pick up eggs, bread, bacon, coffee, and cheese from the grocery store, remember one E, two B's, and two C's. As long as you remember the

correct numbers, you should be able to recall the items in each letter group. This will not only help you memorize the list, but it'll make your shopping experience much faster.

- If you can remember that, among other things, you wanted to buy four different kinds of vegetables, you'll find it easier to remember all four.
- Chunking is what we do when we list a phone number with dashes. Which looks easier to memorize, 8564359820, or 856-435-9820.
- You probably won't remember 17761812184818651898, but try putting a space after every fourth number. Now you can see that those numbers are years, and you can pick key events from each year to help you remember the string of numbers (such as the Revolutionary War, War of 1812, Mexican-American War, Civil War, and Spanish-American War).

4. Use rhymes. Using a variety of common and silly rhymes can help you recall basic information. For example, if you're trying to figure out if April has 30 or 31 days, just say the old rhyme aloud: "Thirty days has September, April, June, and November." Then you'll remember that April does indeed have 30 days. Here are some other rhymes to use as memory tools:

- "In fourteen-hundred ninety-two, Columbus sailed the ocean blue."
- A child can learn the alphabet by singing it to the tune of "Twinkle, Twinkle, Little Star," which makes the letters rhyme.

5. Use acronyms. Acronyms are another wonderful tool for remembering a variety of things, from

the names of the five Great Lakes to the words used as conjunctions. You can use a popular acronym, or create one for yourself. For example, if you're going to the store and know you only need Butter, Lettuce, Bread, and Unagi, then just create a word out of the first letter of each term: "BULB" - Butter, Unagi, Lettuce, and Bread. Here are some popular acronyms to use:

- Homes. This one is used for remembering the Great Lakes: Huron, Ontario, Michigan, Erie, and Superior.
- Roy G. Biv. This man's name can help you remember the colors of the rainbow: Red, Orange, Yellow, Green, Blue, Indigo, Violet.
- Foil. This will help you remember how to multiply two binomial terms: First, Outer, Inner, Last.
- Fanboys. This acronym can help you remember simple coordinating conjunctions: For, And, Nor, But, Or, Yet, So.

6. Use acrostics. Acrostics are similar to acronyms, except instead of just remembering the acronym, you can remember a new sentence made out of the first letters of a set of words that you have to memorize in a certain order. For example, you can say, "My very eager mother just sent us noodles." to learn the order of the planets: Mercury, Venus, Earth, Mars, Jupiter, Saturn, Uranus and Neptune. You can also make up acrostics of your own. Here are a few more popular acrostics:

- Every good boy does fine. This is used for memorizing the lines on the treble music staff: Egbdf.
- Never eat sour watermelons. This is used for remembering the points of a compass in clockwise order: North, East, South, and West. Another good example is Never Eat Shredded Wheat which also rhymes too.
- King philip can only find his green slippers. Use this to memorize the order of the classification system: Kingdom, Phylum, Class, Order, Family, Genus, Species.
- Please excuse my dear aunt sally. Use this to remember the order of operations in mathematics: Parenthesis, Exponents, Multiplication, Division, Addition, Subtraction.

7. Use the method of Loci. This method has been used since the time of Ancient Greece. This technique requires you to associate things in terms of place or location to help you remember the full set of information. To use this method, simply imagine placing the items you want to remember along a route you're very familiar with, or in specific locations in a familiar room or building. First, pick a familiar path; then, picture the things you want to do or memorize along that path.

- If you needed to memorize the acronyms HOMES, FANBOYS, and FOIL, you can picture a miniature home, on your front porch, a loud group of fan boys cheering on your stairs, and some foil wrapped around your bed.
- When you organize a list of information by saying, "in the first place," "in the second place," and so on, you are using a basic version of the method of loci.

Part 2. Using Mindful Approaches

1. Stop thinking that you have a "bad memory." Convince yourself that you do have a good memory that will improve. Too many people get stuck here and convince themselves their memory is bad, that they are just not good with names, that numbers just slip out of their minds for some reason. Erase those thoughts and vow to improve your memory. Celebrate even little achievements to keep yourself motivated.

2. Exercise your brain. Regularly "exercising" the brain keeps it growing and spurs the development of new nerve connections that can help improve memory. By developing new mental skills - especially complex ones such as learning a new language or learning to play a new musical instrument - and challenging your brain with puzzles and games, you can keep your brain active and improve its physiological functioning.

- Try some fun puzzle exercises everyday such as crosswords, Sudoku, and other games which are easy enough for anyone.
- Get out of your comfort zone and pick something that is new and challenging, which makes you flex your brain muscles. Try to play chess or a fast-paced board game.
- A large portion of your brain is activated when it learns a new skill. Learning new information is also helpful, but since skills require both the intake and output of information, they exercise a larger portion of your brain.

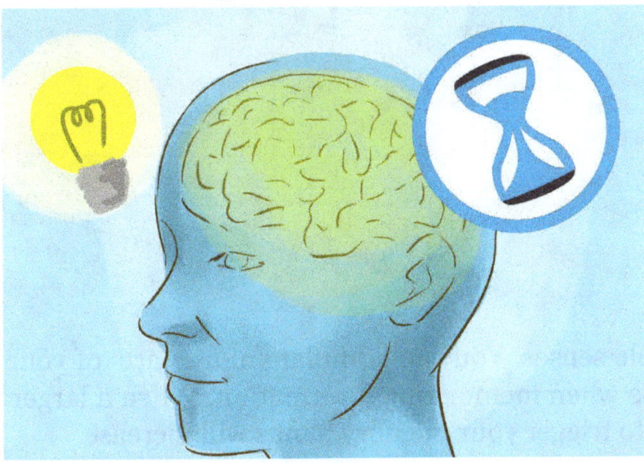

3. Give yourself time to form a memory. Memories are very fragile in the short-term, and distractions can make you quickly forget something as simple as a phone number. The key to avoid losing memories before you can even form them is to be able to focus on the thing to be remembered for a while without thinking about other things, so when you're trying to remember something, avoid distractions and complicated tasks for a few minutes.

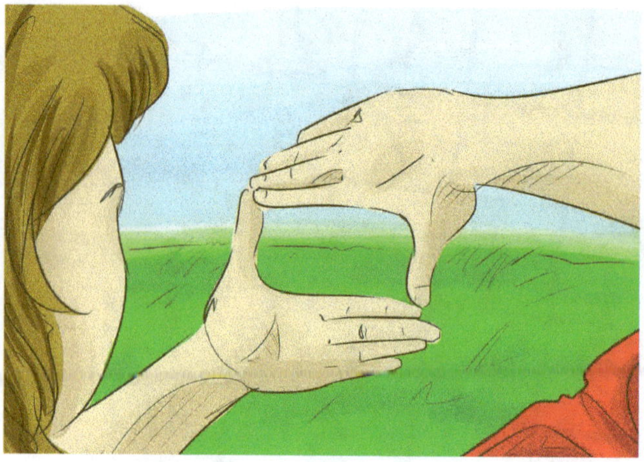

4. Take better pictures. Often we forget things not because our memory is bad, but rather because our observational skills need work. One common situation where this occurs (and which almost everyone can relate to) is meeting new people. Often we don't really learn people's names at first because we aren't really concentrating on remembering them. You'll find that if you make a conscious effort to remember such things, you'll do much better.

- One way to train yourself to be more observant is to look at an unfamiliar photograph for a few seconds and then turn the photograph over and describe or write down as many details as you can about the photograph. Try closing your eyes and picturing the photo in your mind. Use a new photograph each time you try this exercise, and with regular practice you will find you're able to remember more details with even shorter glimpses of the photos.

- 5. Involve multiple senses. You can stimulate more parts of your brain by using as many senses as possible when memorizing information. When a larger part of your brain is active, your ability to trigger your memory banks will increase.
- Write it out. The process of writing information by hand stimulates your brain and makes it easier to remember the information later. Typing is far less effective, however.
- When you do type out information, use a strange font. When you finish, read it back. When something is a struggle to read, you need to concentrate on it more, which can help fix it into your memory more firmly.

- Rehearse or relate the information. Tell yourself or tell another person the information. Hearing yourself recite the information will involve your sense of hearing. If you need to explain the information to the other person so that he or she can understand it, as well, your memory and understanding will be enhanced even further.

6. Use your environment. Change the normal location of things to remember to do something. If you need to remember to take your multivitamins every morning, then put the toaster on its side, and only put it back in its normal place after you've taken your vitamins. Seeing the toaster out of place will remind you that something is off and that there's something you need to remember.

- If you need to remember something important, such as a person's birthday, just wear your wristwatch on your other wrist. You'll remember that there was something important you had to do when you see that the watch is out of position.
- The trick is to focus on what you want to remember as you alter the object being used. If you are not focused on the piece of information, you may not be able to associate it with the change later on.

7. Use flash cards. Flash cards are especially useful for studying. It's essentially a card with a question on one side and the answer on the other. (You can also put two things you want to associate

on opposite sides of a flashcard.) In the course of learning a topic, you would have a stack of cards and would go through them testing yourself. Those that you got right you would put to one side and review a few days later.

- Place the terms you remembered in one pile, and the ones you need to know in another. Keep going until all of the cards are in the "know" pile, even if you need to take breaks.
- Go back to your flash cards the next day and see if you've still memorized the terms on them.

8. Don't cram for an exam. Cramming only works to put information in your short-term memory. You may remember the information for your exam the next day, but you will barely recall the unit when it's time to take the final. Spacing out your studying is important because it gives your brain time to encode the information and store it in your long-term memory.

Part 3. Trying Memory Tricks

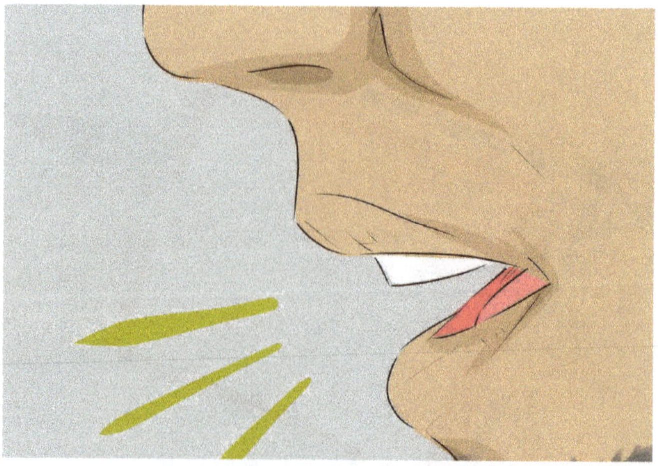

1. Say things you want to remember aloud. If you have trouble remembering whether you took your medication every morning, just say, "I just took my medication." right after you took it, to reinforce this idea in your mind. Saying this aloud will help you remember that you did indeed take your medication.

- This also works if you're meeting a new person and don't want to forget his name. Just repeat the name naturally after you learn it: "Hi, Sarah, it's nice to meet you."
- This also works to remember an address or a meeting time. Just repeat it aloud to the person who invited you: "The Grand Tavern at 7? That sounds perfect."

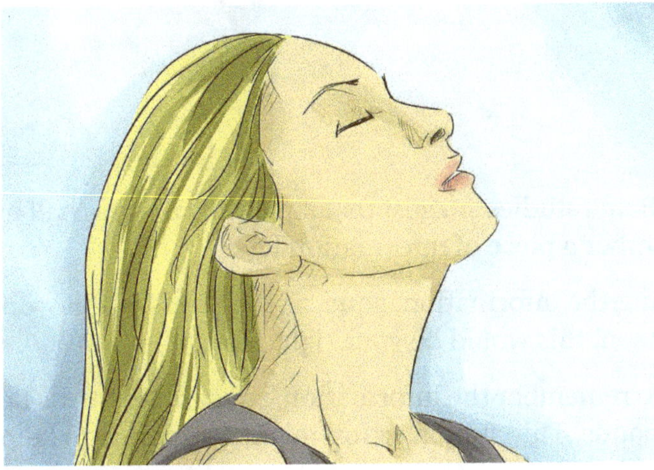

2. Deepen your breathing when you have to remember something. When it's time to study or remember something new, switch your breathing pattern to be slower and deeper. Deeper and slower breathing actually changes the way your brain works, by inducing the brain's electrical pulses to switch to Theta waves, which normally occur in your brain in hypnogogic sleep.

- To activate your Theta waves, switch your breathing to your lower abdomen - in other words, start breathing deeply from your stomach. Consciously slow your rate of breathing too.
- After a few moments, you should feel calmer, the Theta waves should be flowing in your brain, and you should be more receptive to remembering new information.

3. Remember a person's name. Use a popular trick out of FDR's playbook for memorizing a person's name. When a person introduces themselves to you, picture them with their name written on their forehead. This will associate the image of that person with their name.

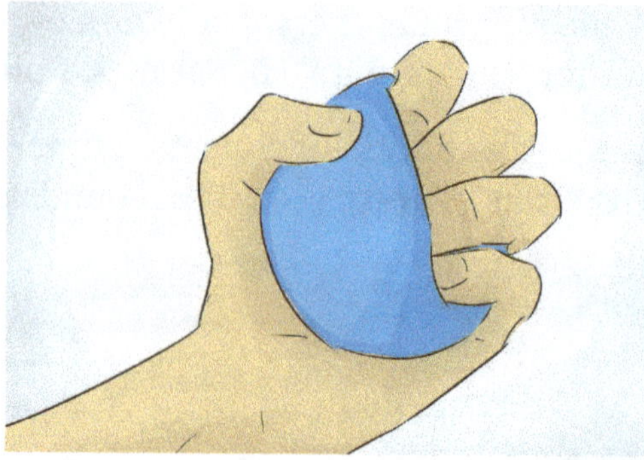

4. Squeeze a stress ball. Some studies suggest that squeezing a stress ball or making a fist with your hand can help you remember a piece of information later.

- Before memorizing the information, squeeze the stress ball in your dominant hand. For a right-handed person, this would be your right hand.
- When you need to remember the information, squeeze the stress ball in your opposite hand for at least 45 seconds. This simple action might be enough to help you remember.

5. Chew gum. This simple act can stimulate the brain and improve your concentration, especially if you need to remember information for 30 minutes or more.

- Some studies have suggested that visual and auditory memory improves when a person chews gum by keeping the individual more focused.
- When you need to remember something for less than 30 minutes, though, it is actually better not to chew anything.

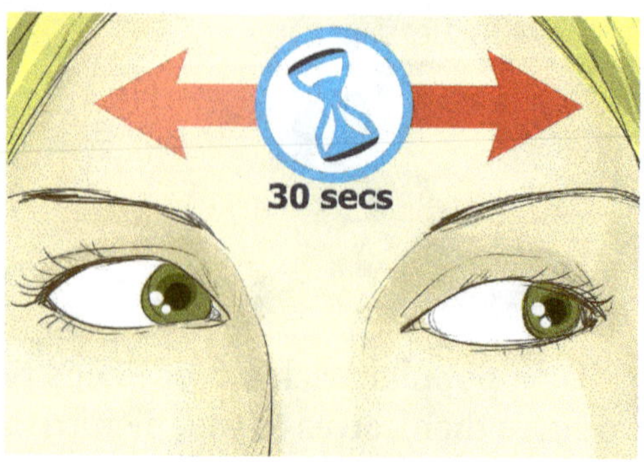

6. Move your eyes from side to side. Studies show that moving your eyes from side to side for just

30 seconds once a day will align the two parts of your brain and make your memory work more smoothly. Try this trick when you wake up in the morning.

7. Smell rosemary. Studies show that smelling rosemary can improve your recall. Carry around a sprig of rosemary or smell rosemary oil once a day. The Ancient Greeks even put a spring of rosemary behind their ears on exam days to help them boost their memories.

8. Try some clever tricks. Begin by memorizing this list of ten words. It's simple - because each word rhymes with its number in the list. When you have to remember a lot of things, use these rhyme-number patterns. For example, you have to remember to clean your glasses. The singular for 'glasses' is 'glass', so just remember this. If this is the first thing on your list, picture a gun, which rhymes with one, shooting the glass. By association the original activity should pop back into your head. The list is enclosed below:

- Gun
- Shoe
- Flea
- Door

- Dive
- Sticks
- Heaven
- Date
- Blind
- Pen

Part 4. Improving your Lifestyle

1. Organize your life. Keep items that you frequently need, such as keys and eyeglasses, in the same place every time. Use an electronic organizer or daily planner to keep track of appointments, due dates for bills, and other tasks. Keep phone numbers and addresses in an address book or enter them into your computer or cell phone. Improved organization can help free up your powers of concentration so that you can remember less routine things.

- Even if being organized doesn't improve your memory, you'll receive a lot of the same benefits (i.e. you won't have to search for your keys anymore).

2. Opt for mindfulness instead of multitasking. Multitasking may seem like it allows you to get things

done faster, but research suggests that it actually causes the brain to slow down overall. Mindfulness allows you to increase your focus, which improves your memory and speeds the brain up.

- You need about eight seconds of focus to commit something to memory. When you multi-task, you tend to set information aside faster than eight seconds, so you're more likely to forget it.
- To practice mindfulness, all you really need to do is improve your concentration and spend more time focusing on one task at a time. When you really want to remember a specific piece of information, spend at least eight seconds focusing on that information alone.

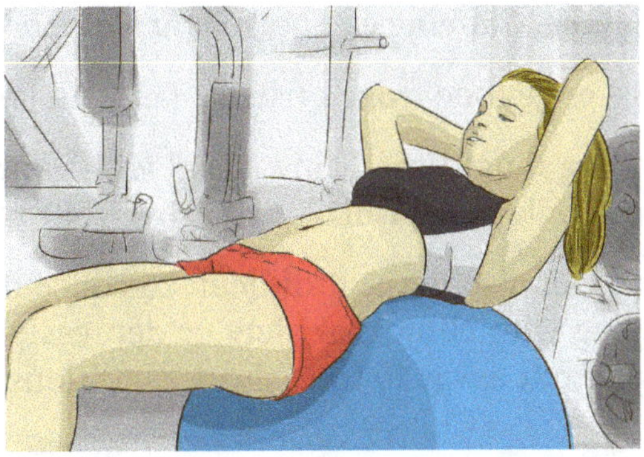

3. Exercise daily. Regular aerobic exercise improves circulation and efficiency throughout the body - including the brain - and can help ward off the memory loss that comes with aging. Exercise also makes you more alert and relaxed, and can thereby improve your memory uptake, allowing you to take better mental "pictures".

- Even just walking for 30 minutes a day is a fantastic form of exercise.
- Nerve cells release neurotropic factors during exercise, and these proteins trigger other chemicals that promote brain health.
- Exercise also improves blood flow to the brain, which increases the amount of oxygen your brain receives.
- Some studies suggest that regular exercise, whether moderate or vigorous, can increase the brain's memory center by one or two percent each year. Without exercise, the memory center will remain stable or may decrease in capacity.

4. Reduce stress. Chronic stress does in fact physically damage the brain, it can make remembering

much more difficult. After prolonged stress, the brain will start to become affected and deteriorate. Stress may never be completely eliminated from one's life, but it definitely can be controlled. Even temporary stresses can make it more difficult to effectively focus on concepts and observe things. Chronic stress can also cause long-term damage to the hippocampus, which is where memories are stored.

- Try to relax, regularly practice yoga or other stretching exercises, and see a doctor if you have severe chronic stress as soon as possible.
- Meditate for at least 15 minutes a day. This will help you slow down your breathing and relax, and it can improve your focus.
- Reduce your caffeine intake. Caffeine can make you feel more anxious and stressed.
- Give yourself a massage or get one from a friend. This will help your body loosen up.
- Reduce stress by spending more time being social with your friends. Being a more social creature and talking to people more will also improve your memory.
- Anxiety and depression can also make it difficult to concentrate and remember information. If you are struggling with clinical anxiety or depression disorders, you should work with your doctor to figure out a way to treat these conditions.

5. Laugh often. Laughter causes multiple parts of your brain to light up, and the portions responsible for your memory are among them.

- Laughing becomes even more beneficial when others are involved. Some studies suggest that socializing with friends, close relatives, and even pets can slow your overall rate of memory decline as you age.

6. Eat well and eat right. There are a lot of herbal supplements on the market that claim to improve

memory, but none have yet been shown to be effective in clinical tests. A healthy diet, however, contributes to a healthy brain, and foods containing antioxidants - broccoli, blueberries, spinach, and berries, for example - and Omega-3 fatty acids appear to promote healthy brain functioning.

- Feed your brain with such supplements as Thiamine, Niacin and Vitamin B-6.
- Some of the suggested foods for your brain are green tea, curry, celery, broccoli, cauliflower, walnuts, crab, chickpeas, red meat, blueberries, and healthy fats (including organic butter, olive oil, coconut oil, nuts, avocado, and salmon or other fatty fish). Each of these foods contains antioxidants that may protect your brain and encourage the production of new brain cells.
- Increase the amount omega-3 fatty acid you consume but decrease omega-6 fats. Omega-3 fats are usually found in salmon and similar animal sources, while omega-6 fats are typically found in processed vegetable oils.
- You should also avoid sugars and grain carbohydrates since these foods can negatively affect your brain. Saturated fats and high-calorie foods are similarly believed to hinder your memory, especially in the long term.
- Red wine may improve your memory when consumed in moderation. If you consume more than one glass a day as a woman or two glasses as a man, the alcohol can begin to impair your memory. In small amounts, though, the resveratrol flavonoid in wine can increase blood and oxygen flow to the brain. Grape juice, cranberry juice, fresh berries, and peanuts are said to provide a similar effect.
- Grazing, or eating 5 or 6 small meals throughout the day instead of 3 large meals, also seems to improve mental functioning (including memory) by limiting dips in blood sugar, which may negatively affect the brain. Make sure it's healthy stuff.

7. Try increasing your vitamin D intake. Studies suggest that low vitamin D may be associated with decreased cognitive performance. When vitamin D receptors in your brain are activated, the nerve growth in your brain increases. Some of the metabolic pathways for vitamin D are located in areas of the brain responsible for forming new memories.

- While too much sunlight can cause skin damage, a moderate amount can provide all the vitamin D needed by the average adult.
- Vitamin D3 supplements are other alternative methods of getting adequate vitamin D.

8. Sleep well. Sleeping improves your neuroplasticity—your brain's ability to grow—which enhances the brain's ability to control behavior and memory. The amount of sleep we get affects the brain's ability to recall recently learned information. Getting a good night's sleep - a minimum of seven hours a night - may improve your short-term memory and long-term relational memory, according to recent studies conducted at the Harvard Medical School.

- Try to get anywhere from 7 to 10 hours of sleep each night. The ideal for most healthy adults is eight hours.
- Go to bed at the same time and wake up at the same time every night. This will make you feel much more rested.
- Spend at least half an hour reading in bed and winding down before you go to bed. Shut off the TV, your computer, and any other visual stimulants at least an hour before bed.
- Take catnaps during the day. They can help you recharge your batteries and boost your memory.
- Your brain also consolidates information into your long-term memory bank during sleep. If you stay awake, this process won't be able to happen.

How to Increase Mental Strength

Mental toughness, like physical toughness, requires that you exercise. Learning to strengthen your mind, improving your concentration, and staying calm will take some work, but you can get the basic skills you need to stay strong of mind.

Part 1. Strengthening your Mind

1. Read everything. Recent studies show that people who enjoy reading novels are more easily able to empathize with others, a sign of a strong and well-rounded mind. If you want to work on increasing your mental strength, read a variety of things that you enjoy.

- You don't have to start from reading unlessly if you want to improve your mental strength, and in fact, trying to read something too difficult might turn you off reading entirely. Instead, focus on reading things you enjoy. Westerns, romance novels, and long-form magazines are all good ways to read.
- Try replacing an hour of television each evening with reading, instead. Invest the time that you might normally spend idling, chatting with friends, or watching the tube in reading a good book.
- Get a library card and take advantage of the library in your town for free entertainment. Try to read one new book every two weeks. Try your best to read from physical books rather than on e-readers.

2. Try to learn something new every week. Ever get the feeling that each day looks a lot the same? As we get older, our mental pathways are more and more defined. Where each summer day seemed to last forever when we were kids, the weeks peel off more quickly as you age. Mental strength requires that you continue building new neural pathways by learning new things.

- Get out of your comfort zone so you can continue to challenge yourself.
- The more regularly you pick up a new skill, or study a new subject, the stronger your mind becomes. Try to pick up one new thing every week, then continue working on it as you learn new things. Build up your mental strength gradually.

3. Socialize more. "Book smarts" are important, but it's also important to understand how things play out in the real world. Social intelligence and wit are important parts of all-around mental health and well-being. If you can't carry on a conversation, work on your social skills along with your mental health building skills.

- Have complicated conversations instead of gossiping. Talk about things that are important to you or things that you've been learning. Try starting or joining a book club in your area.
- Try to meet lots of different kinds of people. If you're in school, don't stick to just one social group, but move around. If you're an adult, try to meet people from socio-economic situations different from your own. Hang out with your plumber, and hang out with your doctor.

4. Challenge yourself. Try things that you're not sure you'll be able to pull off. Decide that you're not only going to learn guitar, but that you're going to learn to shred a fast solo note-for-note.

Decide that you're not only going to play chess, but that you're going to study openings and learn to play like a grandmaster. Keep working on a task until you're at the difficult setting.

- Video games are a mixed bag when it comes to mental strength. Some research shows that video games aid in problem-solving, fine motor skills, logistics, and analysis. Other research points to the negative effects of violence and social isolation associated with video games, decreasing moral sensitivity and attention span.
- Nourish yourself with complex entertainment, and avoid click-bait. If you've ever seen a long newsreel and thought, "Jeez, TLDR" then it's probably time to unplug a little. Reading Buzzfeed or watching YouTube videos of epic fails is like eating three Skittles at lunch. Reading a book or watching a documentary is like eating a meal.

5. Exercise your mind regularly. Just as you can't build muscle by eating cake for three weeks straight before you start lifting at the gym, you can't gain mental strength by goofing off and then focusing only every now and then. Being consistent with brain exercise is more important than the intensity of the workout.

- Even just doing a crossword puzzle or a sudoku every day may decrease your chances of losing mental awareness as you become older while increasing your verbal fluency.

Part 2. Improving Concentration

1. Do one thing at a time. Splitting your attention among multiple tasks makes the quality of

thought that you're giving to each task less. A recent social and psychological study revealed that chronic multi-tasking in a variety of interactive media makes us poorer students, workers, and less efficient learners.

- Start prioritizing the most important things you have to do each day and just focus your attention there. Write out a list to start the day, and work through it.
- Finish one thing before starting another. Even if you find something challenging, stick with it until you're done. Switching between tasks is often more difficult than finishing something you've started.

2. Take frequent short breaks. Recent studies show that as short a break as five minutes every hour results in more efficiency than a single long break in the middle of a workday. Let your brain rest and refresh, to give yourself the best chance of staying mentally strong throughout a difficult task.

3. Get rid of distractions. For lots of people, the chatter of the radio in the background, or the noise of the television is part of almost every minute. If you have a lot of white noise and static in your life, try replacing it with soft relaxing music. Let yourself focus on doing one thing only, instead of trying to entertain yourself while you work.

- Focusing more on what you're doing will have the added benefit of letting you finish your work more quickly. If you're trying to watch a show at the same time, it'll take longer.

- Want to really eliminate distraction? Get off the Internet. When you're trying to study and Facebook is only a click away, it's awfully tempting to mess around. Use a web-blocker or a site-blocker if you can't unplug yourself.
- Leave your phone in another room or on silent so you avoid frequently checking it.

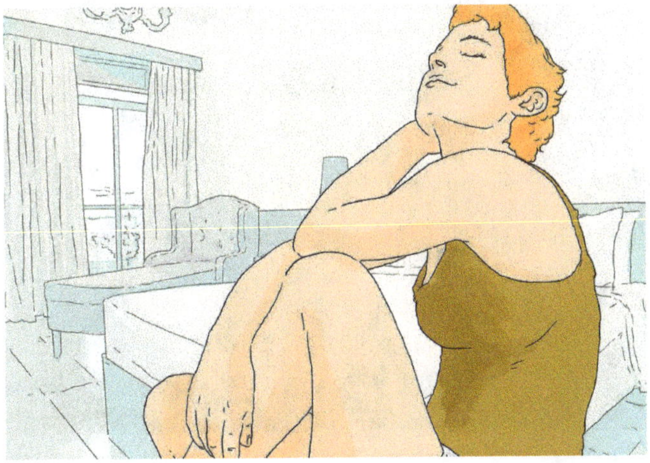

4. Be here now. It may sound overly simple, but one excellent way of focusing your attention back to a task when you find your mind wandering is to remind yourself, "Be here now." Don't think about what you're eating for lunch, or what you're doing later tonight, or what's going to happen this weekend. Just be here now and do what you're doing.

- Try using a keyword mantra, if you don't like "Be here now." Pick a password or a keyword from what you're doing. If you're doing math homework, make it "math" or another related vocab word. When you notice your attention waning, repeat the keyword until you can re-focus.

Part 3. Calming your Mind

1. Be optimistic. Go into each task you perform assuming that you will succeed. Having the right attitude will ensure that your mind is focused in the right places, staying clear of the negative thoughts that can drag you down. Emotional support and strength start within.

- Practice visualization to help with positive thinking. Try actually closing your eyes and "watching" yourself succeed in the task before you. Whatever it is, try to picture yourself doing it correctly and finishing.

2. Let go of petty thoughts. To stay calm and positive, try to let go of petty ego-driven thoughts and concerns, and focus on what's most important. Is what you're wearing important? Is where you're going for dinner? Is what you're going to do this weekend critical to your well-being and mental health? Probably not.

- Stop comparing yourself to other people. It's not good to do better than someone else, or to beat someone else, it's just good to improve your own abilities. Focus on improving yourself, not winning.
- Avoid striving for perfectionism since it can create a lot of pressure on you.

3. Assume the best intentions of others. Don't go looking for something to make you angry or frustrated. Take things at face value and don't over-think your interactions. Your boss probably isn't singling you out and picking on you irrationally. Your friends probably aren't spreading rumors about you behind your back. Stay strong and be confident. You've got this.

- Stay out of other people's business as much as possible. Don't spread gossip or be a collector of gossipy stories. Focus on yourself.

4. Meditate. Taking a bit of time in your day to slow down and focus your thoughts can help you build a strong and calm mind. Meditation doesn't have to be a strange or mystical experience, either. Just find a quiet place and sit for 15-45 minutes each day. That's it.

- Sit comfortably and focus on your breathing. Feel your breath going in and nourishing your body. Feel it leaving your body and entering the world.
- Watch your thoughts come and go without identifying with them. Just let them happen. Stay unattached from them. Focus on your breath.

5. Listen to baroque music. Recent studies have shown that baroque music has the amazing ability to attain a state of deep concentration and focus by preparing alpha brain state in your mind which helps you to boost your learning vocabulary, memorizing facts or reading.

- Select some good baroque music tracks and make a habit of listening to them regularly in your free times or while your working or studying.

6. Do physical exercise as well as mental exercise. Exercise releases endorphins in your brain, which help to calm and strengthen your brain. Getting 30 minutes of exercise a few days a week will help you to stay calmer and more mentally strong. Additionally, one form of exercise that helps the mind relax and can greatly improve mental toughness, is yoga.

How to Increase Mental Stamina

Though endurance is often associated with athletic activities, mentally-grueling projects also require a lot of mental concentration and stamina. Perseverance is of the utmost importance in solving a complex problem. Here are some additional tips to increase your focus and to get tough things done.

Part 1. Improving your Focus

1. Prioritize your tasks efficiently. The better you can organize tasks according to some plan or logic, the more you'll be able to focus and complete those tasks in a timely manner. If you want to improve your mental stamina, improve your prioritizing skills.

- Make a list of what you need to do. Rank the tasks in order of difficulty, or in order of urgency, depending on the tasks.

- Spend five or ten minutes figuring out how much time each task should take, then draw up a quick schedule for yourself and try to stick to it as much as possible.

2. Do one thing at a time. For some people, multi-tasking can work. But if you want to really improve your focus and mental stamina, it's important to narrow in on one thing only, see it through to completion, and then take on something else.

- Start with the most important or the most difficult task you need to accomplish while you're fresh. Get it out of the way, so that the rest of the work you've got to do will be smoother sailing, and will require less of you.
- Do something until it's finished. It takes you a long time to go in and out of tasks, re-acclimating yourself to the job at hand. Instead of getting up and doing something else for a while, finish. Then take a break. Then start something new.

3. Eliminate distractions. If you're focusing on doing math problems, or reading a complicated text, you shouldn't be also trying to eat a sandwich, watch television, or carry on a conversation. Eliminate the noise, put your phone away, and just do the thing you're doing.

- Find a quiet space when you want to focus. If you have trouble finding one where you are, get some noise-canceling headphones and just leave them on silent.
- Lots of people think that the radio on in the background is a good way to study, or that they can watch TV while grading papers. This is partially true. Only listen to music if you've heard it before, and you like it. Don't try to focus on watching a show you've never seen before.

4. Think positively. Self-confidence is one of the most important characteristics to focus and success in a given task. If you go into something that requires great focus, assume that you're going to do well. Assume that you have the skills and the know-how to finish it properly. Assume that you'll succeed.

- Positive thinking is good, but you also have to put the work in. Don't just assume that good vibes will carry you through a tough test. You've still got to study and think hard during the test itself.
- Take deep breaths if you get nervous performing difficult tasks. Focusing on your breathing and calming your nerves will help you perform.

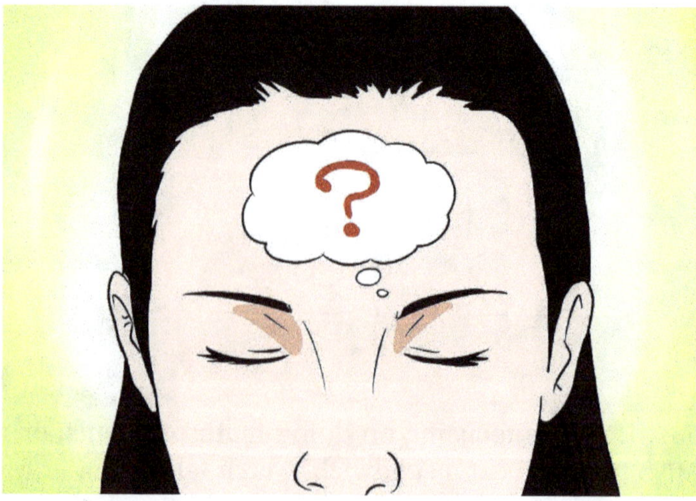

5. Try visualizing. One technique commonly used by athletes involves actually closing your eyes (yes, do this) and picturing what you want to happen in your mind. If you're struggling hard with a test, then picture yourself going through confidently and answering all the questions correctly. Picture your teacher giving you back your tests with the grade you want.

- Do this just before the task itself, and try to stay in that confident head-space. That's where you want to be.

6. Do mental exercises. Playing games that involve your focus and attention can have a positive impact on your ability to focus in the long-term. The ability to assemble lots of different information and come to a conclusion is what focus is all about. Difficult games and mental exercises require you to do just that. Try playing the following types of focus-building games:

- Chess
- Sudoku
- Crossword puzzles
- Turn-based strategy games

- 7. Try to learn new words. Vocabulary building may not seem tied to focus necessarily, but the ability to absorb new information regularly is an important part of overall focus and mental stamina. Make a habit of trying to learn a few new words every month, and keep them rotating in your usage. Be a student of words.
- Learn a new language, if you're feeling really ambitious. Taking on an entirely different vocabulary can open up your mind in exciting ways.

Part 2. Improving your Attention Span

1. Read more. A recent study revealed that people who read novels regularly are able to empathize more easily, and have an easier time paying attention for longer. Head to your local library and pick up some books you're interested in.

- Read everything. You don't have to read heavy classic novels to get the most out of this. Read Westerns or Romance novels. Read the newspaper. Read magazines you like. Read it all.

2. Schedule regular breaks. A recent study revealed that taking regular quick breaks, less than five minutes every hour, is better than taking a single long break in the middle of a difficult task. So, let yourself stop doing what you're doing at least once an hour. Get up, walk around, and turn your mind off for a minute.

- It's usually easier to remember to take one big break, usually for eating, but set a timer to go off every 50 minutes or so, to remind yourself to give yourself a break and do nothing. You need that time.

3. Limit your Internet usage. A Pew Study recently linked the increased availability of high-speed Internet services with a diminished attention capacity in American teenagers. If you're feeling tempted to slap a TLDR on every Facebook post longer than a couple of lines, maybe it's time to give it a break for a while.

- You can also use Internet blockers to help you out if you find the lure of messing around too strong when you're trying to work on your computer.
- Delete unnecessary apps from your phone. You'll spend less time clicking around on Facebook and other social media if you can't do it in transit.

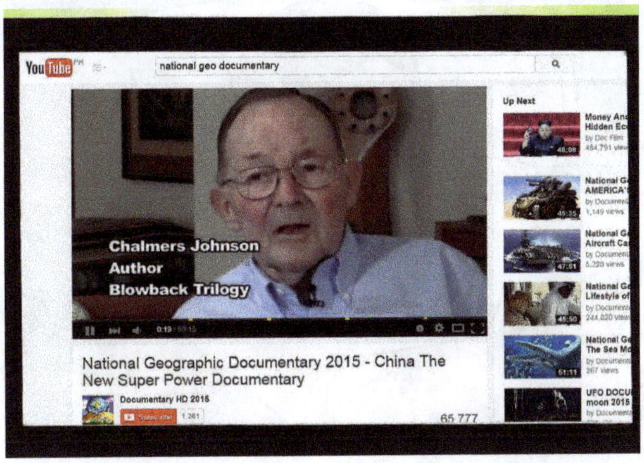

4. Invest in detailed games and stories. Entertainment isn't all equal. Some stuff is difficult to sit through, but learning to appreciate the fun in a long game of chess, or the story told in Anna Karenina can help your attention span improve in other parts of your life. Decide to enjoy something that's slow and quiet, instead of looking for flash-bang fun.

- Watch fewer YouTube clips and short little .gif sites. If you want to sit down and invest in something, watch an engaging movie, documentary, or long-form show that you're interested in.
- You can have fun to, and you don't have to actually like reading Anna Karenina. Mental stamina isn't just an excuse to be pretentious. Form an opinion, but focus and pay attention enough to form that opinion.

5. Don't beat yourself up for slips. Everybody has trouble concentrating sometimes. Even Einstein did. Try not to get too discouraged about your mental stamina, or you risk making it worse. If you're stressed and anxious, your ability to concentrate for a longer period of time with be diminished significantly. Try to relax as much as possible and think positively.

Part 3. Changing your Habits

1. Get more sleep. Sleep gives your brain and body time to recover and rejuvenate. If you want to get the most out of your mind, give it plenty of time to turn off at the end of the day with good-quality rest.

- While most doctors and sleep scientists agree that humans require around 8 hours of sleep per night, individuals differ widely. You know your body best-if waking up in the morning feels like the end of the world, then you're likely not getting enough.
- Don't eat, or drink any caffeine, alcohol, or sugary beverages shortly before bed. When your body's working to digest, your sleep suffers in quality.

2. Change your diet. What you put into your body affects the way your mind works. If you've got a day of heavy lifting in the brain department, make sure you eat a diet rich in protein, slow-digesting carbohydrates, and fresh fruits and vegetables to get your brain firing on all cylinders.

- Oatmeal, fruit, cereal, toast, and yogurt are all great breakfast choices if you've got to do some heavy thinking over the course of a day. Of course, if you're a coffee drinker, it's fine to have a cup-but stop after one.
- Avoid heavy saturated fats, sugary foods, and high caffeine levels. Over-doing the caffeine will almost certainly cause you to crash, and the first thing to suffer will be your mental stamina. Cut back on caffeine if you're a regular user.

3. Drink plenty of water. 70% of your body is water and your body requires lots of it to function. Try to drink as much as two liters of water a day, to make sure that your body and its organs are being replenished and rejuvenated.

4. Do physical exercise as well as mental. Get your body moving to help get your mind clear. There

are direct connections between exercise and mood, and exercise releases positive mood hormones in your brain that helps you stay positive and upbeat, an essential part of focus.

- Use exercise as a break, or as a way to meditate. Just going on a short brisk walk after meals can be a great way of getting a little exercise.

5. De-stress regularly. Your mind needs both exercise and an occasional break. If you tend toward the obsessive, or have trouble shutting your brain off, it can make it very challenging to focus. You don't have to be on all the time. Give yourself permission to relax your mind and calm your stress.

- Try progressive muscle relaxation regularly, especially if you're in the middle of something tough. It only takes fifteen minutes, and involves nothing more than slowly tensing and releasing your muscles.
- Consider meditation. Yoga, deep breathing, and other types of simple relaxation techniques can also be quite effective.

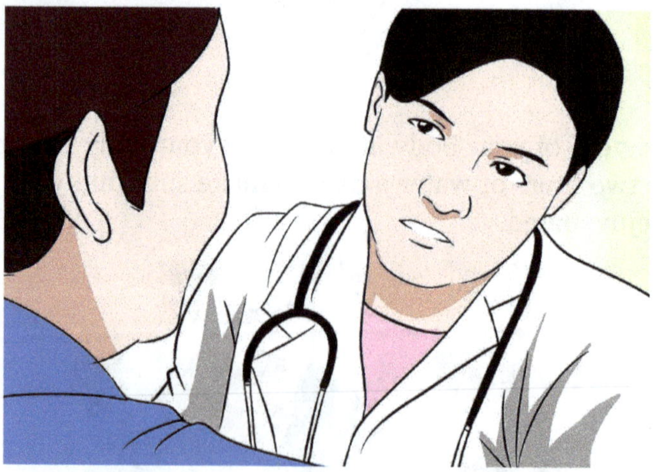

6. Talk to your doctor if you struggle to pay attention. If you think that your peers are consistently outperforming you in mental stamina, focus, and concentration and that it is a problem in your life, consider talking to your doctor about testing for learning disabilities or ADHD. You might be eligible for a prescription to a stimulant medication to help you concentrate.

- Psychostimulants don't work for everyone, and side effects can vary depending on the person. It may take a while to get used to the drug.

How to Exercise your Brain for Better Thinking Skills

Not so very long ago, scientists and doctors believed that the number of neurons, cells, and pathways that were present in our brains at birth were pretty much all there would be, so we should "use it or lose it", as the saying goes. Your brain consists of four primary lobes, convoluted structures found within the lobes, left and right hemispheres, intricate communication networks, and more than 100 billion neural cells. The good news is, in recent years, the scientific research community has discovered a process called neuroplasticity. This means that the neuronal communication pathways and neural cells in the brain continue to grow throughout all the years of our lives. The process slows as we age, but it doesn't stop completely as was once believed. Stimulating the growth of new neural cells and pathways to improve your thinking skills and your overall brain function can be done.

Part 1. Exercising your Brain

1. Grow new neurons. Your brain is filled with literally billions of cells that contain a cell nucleus, axons, dendrites, and synapses.

- One proven way to grow new neurons is to learn. The existing axons, dendrites, and synapses, need to be maintained so don't get lazy. Continue to perform the things you already do, including sports, reading, puzzles, exercise, crafts, or music.
- The key to growing new neurons is to teach yourself something different, maybe even something that feels awkward at first.
- Neuroplasticity of the brain, or the ability to grow new brain cells, happens if you take charge and expose your brain to something different.

2. Try something new. Learn to juggle, dance, play a musical instrument, or anything that is new to you.

- Even doing familiar things in a different way can help. For example, navigate your way through your home, safely, while walking backwards.
- Try anything you can think of that creates a challenge for your brain, but it must be something that requires you to think.

3. Perform neurobic exercises. Neurobics are exercises designed to stimulate new growth in the brain. The primary basis of neurobics involves using the senses to stimulate new brain pathways. Think of ways to challenge your brain by altering your sensory perceptions. Some basic examples follow:

- Get dressed in the morning with your eyes shut or a blind-fold on.
- Wear headphones that suppress sound while trying to verbally communicate with a friend. Include speaking and trying to understand what they are saying by mouth movements and hand gestures.
- If you play the piano, try playing a simple and familiar piece with your eyes shut, or with two fingers taped together.
- Try playing a simple piece using all fingers, but play the bass clef using your right hand and above middle C, and the treble clef with your left hand and below middle C.

- Use your non-dominant hand for routine activities. Try brushing your teeth, combing your hair, and using a computer mouse using your non-dominant hand.
- Write with your non-dominant hand.
- Try writing several sentences from memory, perhaps the first verse of a familiar poem or song, making the letters upside down, as a mirror image, or from right to left on the page.
- Try playing your favorite sport using your non-dominant hand.
- Break your routines. Put your shoes on in the opposite order. Mow the yard in the opposite direction. Think of other frequent routines and alter their order.
- Go for an early morning walk simply to identify smells around you.
- Try to identify the ingredients in a meal just from taste and smell.

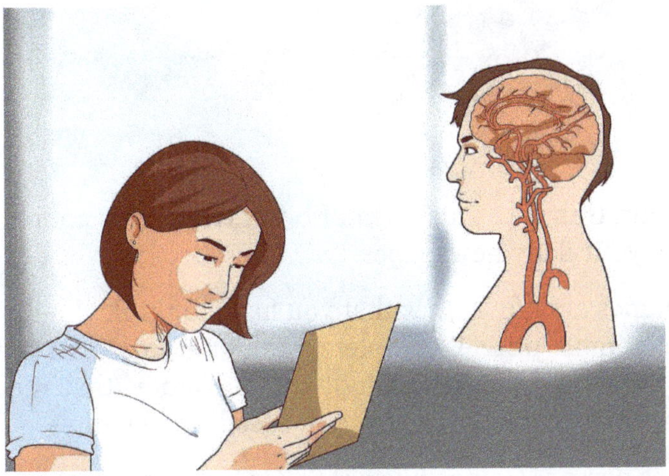

4. Improve whole brain blood flow. A recent study used only strategy-based brain training, without introducing any elements of physical exercise, to improve blood flow in the brain. The results showed that whole brain blood flow was significantly increased by using only brain-training exercises.

- The point of the study was to increase whole brain blood flow using only mental exercises.
- When blood flow to the brain slows down, atrophy of brain tissues results. Atrophy in the brain means that cells degenerate, important communicate pathways degrade, and the brain tissue and important structures shrink away.
- The study enrolled people of all ages that had suffered a traumatic brain injury, with about 65% of the enrollees having suffered the brain injury at least 10 years prior.
- Part of the group was exposed to strategy-based brain training, and the others were exposed to general teaching materials, for the same amount of time, about how the brain works.
- The group that received the strategy-based training improved abstract thinking scores by more than 20%, memory function measures improved by 30%, and the whole brain blood flow showed a significant increase as compared to the control group.

- Many of the group participants also suffered from symptoms of depression and post-traumatic stress disorder. Depressive symptoms were improved in the strategy-based training group by 60% and post-traumatic stress disorder symptoms improved by almost 40%.
- Strategy-based brain training really works to increase whole brain blood flow and can help to prevent brain shrinkage.

5. Try strategy-based brain training. This form of brain training is common and can be found all around you, including in your daily newspaper.

- Strategy brain games are any games that you have to think about to solve. Do a crossword puzzle, a word-scramble puzzle, complete a Sudoku puzzle, or put together an actual table-top puzzle. Puzzle games that are not left to chance, that require you to think about them to solve them, are considered strategy-based brain games.
- Play with another person. Games like chess, Go, or even checkers, involve thinking about your moves, and anticipating the moves of the person you are playing against.

6. Boost your brain by using mental exercises. Make a list of something you commonly do, like a grocery list or things to do that day, and memorize the list.

- A few hours after you have completed the list, or even the next day, try to remember everything on it.

7. Perform math calculations in your head. Start simple and systematically.

- As you get more comfortable with the easier problems, work your way into harder math. Make it even more interesting by taking a walk while you do the calculations in your head.

8. Create pictures of words in your head. Visualize a word, then create a way to challenge yourself using that word.

- One way is to think of other words that start and end with the same letters, or think of words that have more syllables than the first one but still rhyme.

9. Participate in making music. The musical experience is a valuable one. Do something musical that you are not accustomed to doing.

- If you already play an instrument, learn to play a different one.
- Join a singing group. Even if you cannot sing well, joining a choir or vocal group will significantly expand your brain function on several levels.
- You will learn to understand organization of the music on the pages you will be singing, timing and rhythm, and organized singing. Plus, you will be exposed socially to a new group of people which provides a wonderful opportunity to expand your brain even further as you learn about music.

10. Take a class. Try a cooking class, auto mechanics, wood-working, sewing, or crafting.
    - Taking a class in something that you do not know how to do, but are interested in learning, helps to develop new pathways in your brain.
    - This happens both by learning the new material and interacting with new people in a new environment.

11. Learn a new language. This is a very good way to improve cognitive function and thinking ability.
    - New languages also help to expand your vocabulary which is associated with higher cognitive functioning. Plus, hearing and speaking a new language develops new pathways in your brain.

12. Learn a new sport. Try a sport that is new to you, and consider one that involves at least one other player.

- Golf is a sport that you can basically play alone, but it is more challenging when you play with someone. This creates additional experiences for your brain to organize and react to, and therefore the growth of new brain cells and pathways result.

13. Talk to people. The more conversations you have, the more your brain has to work in order to compensate and process the new information.

- If you have children, have conversations with them. The more conversations you have with your child, the smarter they will be.

14. Develop friendships with a diverse group. Having conversations on topics with people that

have very different opinions challenges your brain, and your executive function abilities, to determine how you respond to the same topic but in different groups.

- The more diverse your friends are, the more your brain is challenged to become creative both in conversation and in participation of different types of social interactions.

Part 2. Exercising your Body to Improve your Thinking Skills

1. Participate in aerobic exercise. More and more research points to physical exercise as the most effective way to improve thinking skills and overall brain function.

- Create an exercise routine that includes one hour sessions, three times a week, and basic exercises like walking on a treadmill or riding a stationary bike.
- Stay with your exercise routine for at least 12 weeks in order to improve your brain fitness, cognitive abilities, and thinking skills.
- A recent study done in sedentary people, aged 57 to 75 years of age, supports this level of exercise with scientific data.
- The exercise group showed rapid improvement in circulating blood flow to areas of the brain, significant improvement in both immediate and delayed areas of memory function, improved cognitive abilities, frontal lobe functioning, visuospatial skills, processing speed, and overall improved cognition. Cardiovascular measures included as part of the study design were also notably improved.
- The authors interpret the study results as further indication that any person, at any age, can take steps through the use of physical exercise to positively influences brain neuroplasticity.

2. Integrate exercise with your study habits. Recall of vocabulary words was significantly improved

when exercise was included just before, during, or immediately after, exposure to the vocabulary words.

- Two different studies, one in female college students, and one in male college students, validated much improved recall of vocabulary words studied when associated with exercise.
- The female students did the best when they were exposed to their vocabulary words for 30 minutes while they were also exercising. The form of exercise in this study was riding a stationary bicycle for 30 minutes.
- The male students were divided into groups that included no exercise, moderate exercise, or vigorous exercise. The improvement was noted in the students that were exposed to their vocabulary words either immediately prior, or immediately after, vigorous exercise.

3. Exercise to increase your BDNF levels. Cognitive function and memory recall is improved when a substance called brain-derived neurotrophic factor, or BDNF, is elevated.

- Exercise increases you levels of BDNF.
- Your BDNF levels fall back to normal ranges approximately 30 minutes after stopping your exercise routine so take advantage of that time. Tackle a difficult project from work or study for an exam as soon as you can following your exercise routine.

4. Start exercising now; the younger the better. Structures within our brain perform different functions and communicate through complex networks to keep our thinking skills sharp and memory function

stable, help make critical decisions, strategize ways to solve problems, process and organize incoming information, keep our emotions in check, and control how we respond to countless situations.

- When structures in the brain lose volume, or start to shrink, our brain function declines along with the parts of the brain that are shrinking. Exercise helps to prevent shrinkage.
- The prefrontal cortex and hippocampus, structures in the brain that support memory function and higher-level cognitive functions, begin to shrink at a rate of about 1% to 2% each year for people over the age of 55 years.
- Research done in 2010 showed the first documented evidence that exercising early in life helps to prevent shrinkage in the brain in later years, reducing the risk of cognitive decline.

5. Get up and move. The scientific community is still working to determine the best exercises to do, and how long to do them, in order to provide the greatest improvement in brain function. While that question remains unanswered, some things have become clear.

- Stretching and muscle tone exercises do very little to nothing to improve brain function.
- Whatever you do, it needs to be something that requires active participation.
- Walking on a treadmill and riding a stationary bicycle count as actively participating.
- This type of aerobic exercise helps not only to maintain brain abilities but can actually help to recover abilities that may be fading away. Even when the aging process, medical conditions, and even brain injury, are working against you, exercising is your proven way to fight back.
- So get up and move. Walk using a treadmill or a calculated and safe path, ride a stationary bicycle or a regular one if safety permits, and possibly even participate in competitive sports like tennis.
- Competitive and active sports, such as tennis, may provide even greater benefit since other areas of the brain are engaged. The additional parts of brain exposure involve socializing, problem-solving, visuospatial reaction, anticipation, and reaction times.

6. Improve your cognitive flexibility. Cognitive flexibility allows us to think about more than one thing at the same time, to rapidly switch your activity and your thoughts from one topic to another, and to quickly adapt to changing situations.

- Active and persistent exercise, specifically running, has been associated with significant improvements in cognitive flexibility.

Part 3. Stimulating your Frontal Lobe

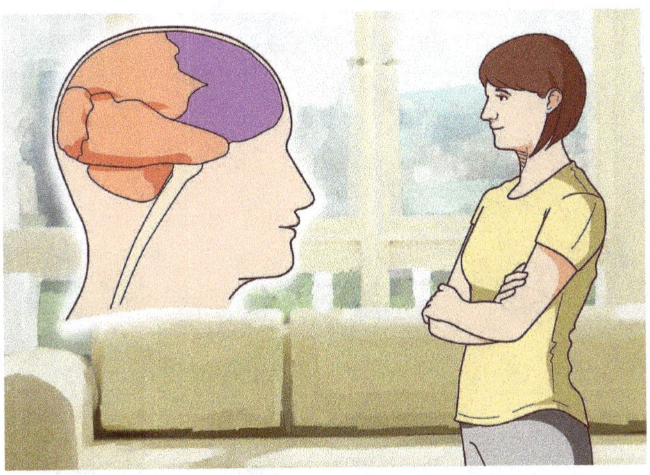

1. Think of your frontal lobe as your central command. Your frontal lobe is the largest of the four lobes and is the area responsible for higher level cognitive function.

- The frontal lobe is the center of your executive function and also integrates communication throughout the rest of your brain in order to carry out your executive function decisions.
- Executive function abilities are needed for organizing the information that is coming into the brain and to regulate how your respond.
- Examples include time management, attention processes, multi-tasking and switching focus, being detail oriented when needed, controlling what you say and do, and making decisions based on you own prior experiences.

2. Play. Both physical play as exercise and gentle play with a child, friend, or family member helps to strengthen the frontal cortex and the processes involved with executive function.

- Physical play helps to sharpen your executive function skills as you anticipate and react to constantly changing situations.

3. Use your imagination. Imaginative play helps to strengthen executive function ability as your brain works to strategize your reaction to the unknown circumstances and situations you are creating in your mind.

- Think of positive scenarios and develop them into stories, or chapters within a story.
- Find images in the clouds, imagine a conversation between ducks and fish, create a painting in your head of your favorite song, or do anything that engages your imagination.
- Using your imagination stimulates your brain to release chemicals that are rewarding and engaging. Firing brain neurons along axons, dendrites, and synapses, that are seldom used is key in growing new ones.

4. Avoid negative influences. While it is important to address situations that are difficult, try to avoid allowing the negativity to persuade the way you think and feel.

- Some people and situations can be very dramatic. Keep a positive and problem-solving attitude when faced with negative circumstances.

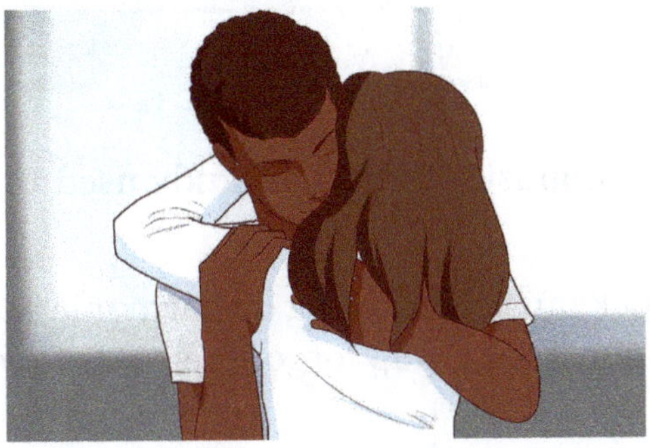

5. Give a hug. Forms of physical contact, such as giving and receiving hugs, and other physical gestures of support and friendship, provide a calming effect on the brain.

- Positive social interactions are healthy and can help to develop new pathways in your brain when you are in an unfamiliar, yet positive, situation. Social interaction is important to creating new brain pathways.
- Your brain is constantly learning and utilizing executive function skills as you interact with other people, formulate your response to situations, and consider possible reactions of the other person and react accordingly.

6. Listen to music. Music has been clearly shown to cause changes, both positive and negative, in the frontal lobe of the brain.

- Exposure to music has been proven as an aid to improve your IQ and enhance the ability to learn. Reading and literacy skills improve, spatial-temporal reasoning is enhanced, and mathematical abilities are improved.
- Some styles of music has been tied to bad outcomes, including unhealthy lifestyle choices, criminal activity, and even suicidal behavior.
- Other styles of music are linked to early development of visuospatial abilities, better math performance, improved ability to learn a foreign language, and an overall healthy lifestyle.

7. Review the results from a rock music study. The study used three groups of mice exposed to different music styles.

- The group exposed to rock music, including disharmonic beats, behaved in a disorganized, confused, and lost manner. That group forgot their way to food in a maze they had already located.
- Two other groups, one exposed to only classical music and one to no music at all were able to find their way through the maze to the food, actually performing even faster.
- With further study, the scientists found frontal lobe shrinkage and hippocampal damage in the group exposed to the rock music with disharmonic beats.
- While several studies suggest that rock music, or possibly the binaural beats within rock music, has a negative influence, other research supports music of choice, including rock music, as a good way to engage your brain and develop additional neuronal pathways.

Part 4. Expanding your Critical Thinking Ability

1. Accept the challenge. Improving your critical thinking skills is a commitment to yourself. This is a process that takes time.

- Critical thinking is a method of analyzing, evaluating, and making decisions. Most people take thinking for granted and overlook the need to evaluate thinking habits and develop new and positive ways to critically evaluate and react to daily circumstances.
- Realize that it takes both time to evaluate, change, and develop critical thinking skills, and practice to arrive at the level you want. Just as a professional athlete or musician continues to sharpen their talents and abilities, you can work to sharpen your thinking skills.
- Improving your critical thinking ability requires approaching information and decision making by avoiding prejudice, over-generalization, common fallacies or pre-determined beliefs, deception, and rigidity and narrowness in your thinking.
- Doing things that are concrete helps to bring your thinking processes to light, and helps you to make changes that improve your critical thinking. Any one step can be helpful, but actively and routinely practicing changes over time improves your thinking ability.

2. Make use of wasted time. Avoid flipping through channels, getting frustrated while sitting in traffic, worrying unproductively, and jumping from one activity or diversion to another without enjoying anything.

- Use that valuable time to ask yourself questions that can improve your approach to the next day. Ask questions that help you evaluate what you did well that day, or not so well. Consider your strengths and weaknesses of the day so far.
- If possible, record your answers so you can develop your thoughts in those areas even further.

3. Solve a problem each day. Set aside problems that are out of your control, and focus on the tools you need and the steps to take to solve problems within your control.

- Avoid becoming overwhelmed or emotional and work through the problem in an organized, logical, and thoughtful manner.
- Consider factors like short-term solutions as opposed to long-term solutions, the advantages and disadvantages of the solutions you are considering, and develop a workable strategy to solve the problem.

4. Focus your thoughts each week on one intellectual standard. Accepted intellectual standards include clarity of thought, precision, accuracy, relevance, depth, breadth, logical factors, and significance.
    - For example, during the week you focus on clarity you may want to think about how clearly you communicated something during a meeting or in a conversation with your spouse or a friend. Think about ways you might have improved on your clarity.
    - Also consider how clear others have communicated information to you, or to a group.
    - Clarity in writing is just as important. Evaluate your own written communications, those of others, and in published literature.

5. Journal. Follow a pattern to your journaling, and make several entries each week.
    - Write about situations in which you were involved, how you responded, your analysis of things apparent and hidden in the situation, and an assessment of what you learned about yourself in the process.

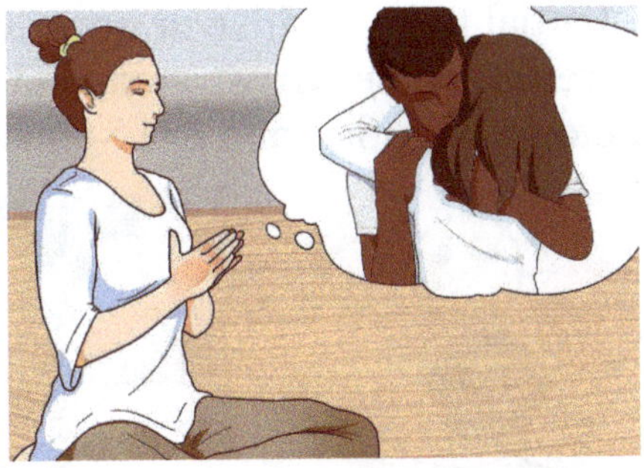

6. Reshape your character. Focus on one intellectual trait each month, including perseverance, autonomy, empathy, courage, humility, and any other traits you may admire in others but find lacking in yourself.

- Think about each trait and develop a strategy to improve that trait in yourself. Possibly include your progress in your journal.
- Keep your focus on your selected trait throughout the month. Continually evaluate your performance noting improvement, setbacks, and additional work needed.

7. Face your own egocentric thinking. Placing bias on yourself is a natural way of thinking.

- Ask yourself questions to help identify situations where you may have placed too much emphasis on your own opinion. Include questions that help you evaluate any actions you may have taken based on irritability over unimportant or small things, saying or doing things irrationally to push things your way, or situations where you imposed your own will or opinion on others.
- Once you recognize your egocentric reactions, take steps to modify your thinking to correct those behaviors.

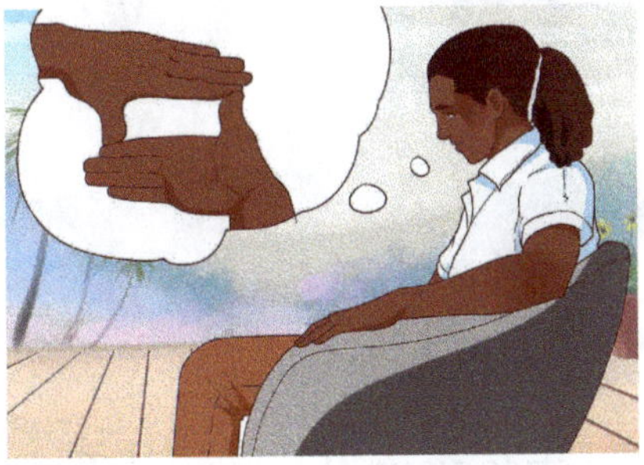

8. Adjust the way you see things. Practice seeing the good in difficult or negative situations.

- Every situation has the potential to be positive or negative. Seeing the positive in a situation leads one to feel more rewarded, less frustrated, and overall happier. Take the opportunity to turn mistakes into opportunities, and dead-ends into beginnings.

9. Recognize your emotional reactions. Evaluate situations or thoughts that cause you to feel angry, sad, frustrated, or upset.

- Take the opportunity to explore what is causing your negative emotion and find a way to turn that into a positive reaction.

10. Review groups that influence your life. Groups have a way of suggesting certain beliefs or behaviors that are "better" than others.

- Analyze the groups in your own life that influence your decisions and your actions. Consider pressures placed on you by the group and evaluate those pressures as being positive or negative. Consider how you can adjust your own reaction to negative pressures without damaging relationships or altering the group dynamic.

11. Think about how you think. Practice your thinking skills and develop your critical thinking ability.

- Develop and implement strategies that use your personal experiences in order to further influence and develop your critical thinking skills.

Part 5. Using Diet and Supplements to Improve your Brain Function

1. Eat a healthy diet. A recent research evaluated the diet in 550 seniors. The study authors were only looking for evidence of a link between diet and brain function.

- The researchers found more than what they were looking for. The study revealed that eating a healthy diet actually improves executive functioning in the frontal lobe.
- The results also strongly suggest that eating a healthy diet can shield the brain against aging processes that lead to dementia and Alzheimer's disease.
- Study participants that had the best scores also were more interested in physical activity and in avoiding habits like smoking.

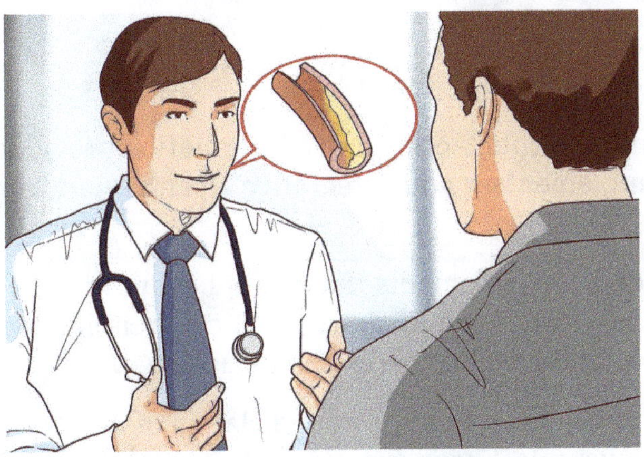

2. Monitor your cholesterol. While cholesterol levels have not been directly tied to brain function, people with lower cholesterol levels have stable blood flow which allows the oxygen in the blood to be effectively carried to the brain for optimal function.

- Talk to your doctor about your cholesterol levels. There may be ways to effectively address any levels that are not within the normal range. Interventions recommended by your doctor can include both prescription medications as well as non-medication options.

- Some study participants showed results as high as 66% reduction in the odds of developing poor executive function based solely on healthy levels of saturated fat intake which contributes to lower cholesterol levels.

3. Prevent medical conditions that cause cognitive decline. Beyond the brain function values, researchers concluded that maintaining a healthy diet can prevent conditions that lead to slower thinking, cognitive decline, and lower executive functioning abilities.

- Some medical conditions known to contribute to an overall decline in brain function include cardiovascular disease, diabetes, vascular disease, and obesity.

4. Know the facts about supplements. According to information provided by the National Institute of Health's Center for Complementary and Integrative Health, many products are claiming benefits that do not exist.

- Scientific evaluations of supplements that claim benefit in improving brain function, preventing memory loss, improving memory function, treating dementia, or slowing Alzheimer's disease, reveal those claims to be unsubstantiated.
- To date, there is no evidence to support the claims of efficacy that any dietary or herbal supplement can prevent decline in functioning or improve problems in memory function. This includes products such as ginkgo, omega-3 fatty acids, fish oil, vitamins B and E, Asian ginseng, grape seed extract, and curcumin.
- While there is no evidence to support any claims of efficacy of these products, scientists are continuing to study some of these agents to determine if there is any possible benefit.
- Research involving mindfulness techniques and music therapy is ongoing, with preliminary results showing some promise in these areas.

5. See your doctor as soon as you notice symptoms. Do not delay in seeing your doctor while you attempt to try other approaches.

- While some approaches may be helpful to your condition, your physician can provide a tremendous amount of information that may direct your care in a manner that has proven results.
- Many complementary approaches that include herbal medicines and some vitamin products can seriously interact with prescription strength medications.
- Talk to your doctor before you try any products to treat symptoms of decline in cognitive abilities or evidence of memory loss.

How to Stay Mentally Strong

Enjoying strong mental health means understanding the meaning of well-being, functioning normally in everyday life, and having enough confidence to overcome the hurdles that confront you on a daily basis. In many ways, mental health is no different than physical health in that actions can be taken to promote a healthy mind. It is important to take care of your mental health from childhood through adulthood in order to avoid depression, anxiety, excessive stress, and addiction, conditions that can impact anybody. Having a peaceful mind should always be an important goal throughout life.

Method 1. Building Relationships

1. Connect with friends and family. These are the people who love and care about you and will be

the most honest. Whatever emptiness you have can be filled by the friends and family who will provide you comfort and confidence. It is important to balance your life between work, fun, and family.

- Talking with people you love and trust is a good way to relieve stress, think positive, and take your mind off of work and other pressing issues.
- Regardless of how busy your weekly schedule is, take one day of the week to dedicate to friends and family. Your body and mind will appreciate it.
- Family and friends also provide companionship, camaraderie, and happier encounters that reduce feelings of loneliness and stress.

2. Socialize with people who share similar interests. Communicating with people who enjoy similar activities creates a sense of belonging and promotes mental health.

- Join a gym, book or card club, a sports team, or an evening walk group, to not only enjoy physical and mental exercise but also to get out of the house.
- Cultivate friendships with intelligent, educated, and experienced people. These friendships will produce stimulating conversations on a variety of topics exposing you to new ideas, perspectives, and understandings, which is a good mental exercise.
- You can locate these clubs and organizations in many places such as online, the classified section of the newspaper, or through friends and family members.

3. Volunteer in your community. Participating in volunteer activities has shown to increase one's

well-being, self-confidence, and self-esteem. Volunteering often benefits the community, giving you a sense of unity, accomplishment, and a positive outlook on life.

- Volunteering does not have to be a major undertaking. Instead, help out an elderly neighbor get groceries, shovel the driveway in winter for a single mother, or plant a community garden to promote the health of others.
- Biologically, the side effect of making social connections through volunteering is the release of the hormone oxytocin, which is associated relaxation, trust, and psychological stability.

Method 2. Enjoying Life

1. Find a hobby. Make time throughout the week to engage in activities you enjoy doing. Make it a point to relax and have fun without much stress. Hobbies, for example, are a great excuse to take a break from your busy lifestyle but still have a sense of purpose in doing them.

- Studies show that a rush of excitement or joy, such as taking a walk, playing with your dog, or cooking, releases eustress, a moderate psychological stress shown to be beneficial for you.
- As a positive break from work, hobbies offer new challenges for your brain and an outlet for stress. Focusing on activities different from work gives your mind new tasks to focus on.
- The intensity of participating in something you enjoy makes time fly by. This is time you are not dwelling on the past or worrying about the future.
- Engaging in activities that you love have proven to lower blood pressure, cortisol, obesity, and body mass index while, at the same time, increasing levels of positive psychosocial states. This proves that hobbies are good for mind, body, and soul.

2. Stay active. Exercise is good for your body, but it is also good for your mental health. Many stud-

ies link increased self-esteem, concentration, and physical appearance with exercising. Exercising also improves sleep, energy levels, and social engagement while decreasing tension, stress, and mental fatigue.

- No need for an expensive gym membership. Instead, take a jog in the park, a swim in the ocean, lake, or river, or stretch in the living room. There are many ways to remain active outside the gym or even at work.
- Moderate exercise – breathing heavier than normal or just breaking a sweat – for thirty minutes five times a week is recommended by most physicians.
- Choose activities that fit into your daily schedule, times that work for you, and make it a lifestyle commitment.
- If you need a partner to keep you motivated, ask a colleague, friend, or family member to join you.

3. Eat Healthy. Eating healthy is essential for strong mental health. Not doing so will only encourage a range of possible mental health illnesses. Recent studies show that the types of food you eat will determine whether you are more prone to mental health problems or not. In short, eat a balanced diet that emphasizes lots of fruits and vegetables.

- Try to eat three healthy meals every day to control your blood sugar levels. Missing meals, especially breakfast, will cause you to be hungrier, irritable, and fatigued throughout the day. Eat a healthy snack to make up for it if you have to.
- Concentrate on reducing refined foods such as sugar and increasing whole grains, fruits, and vegetables. Sugar will give you a surge of energy but ultimately will leave you tired and irritable while the sugar in fruits is absorbed slower and keeps your mood balanced.
- Protein is full of the amino acid tryptophan, which reduces anxiety and stress, regulates behavior, and improves the quality of sleep. Make sure your brain is fed a steady diet of tryptophan by including meat, fish, eggs, cheese, and nuts in your regular meal plan.
- Omega-3 and omeg-6 fatty acids found in fish oils should also find its way into your diet because they play an important role in normal brain development and function, and are known to help prevent heart attacks, strokes, and cancers.

- Drink lots of water to stay hydrated and avoid excessive alcohol to prevent dehydration. Dehydration causes irritability, loss of concentration, and reduced mental power, which is also found in the side effects of alcohol.
- Keep your diet diversified and interesting so that you can ensure you are getting the complete range of vitamins, minerals, and nutrients your body and mind need to function at a high level.
- Maintain a healthy weight to control your mood and self-esteem.
- Avoid taking drugs. Substance abuse is not a solution to solving your problems. Taking drugs only creates problems.

4. Practice good sleeping habits. Sleeping for eight hours a day will restore your mind and body while preparing you for the next day. Without adequate sleep, your mental health will suffer, your concentration will be short, and you will be easily agitated.

- Try to go to bed and wake up at the same time every day. Good habits will result in better sleeping patterns since your body will become used to the routine.
- If you do not get enough sleep, then find five or ten minutes to relax your brain by letting your mind wander, daydream, or meditate during the day.

5. Ask for help. Do not be afraid to rely on others during stressful times. Whether that is dropping the kids off at mom's house for a break or letting the kids sleep over at the neighbor's house.

- Always try to ask somebody you trust and can count on. This will bring you comfort and ease your mind.
- True strength and understanding comes from utilizing your resources – friends and family – when you need them. It is not a sign of weakness or failure to ask for help. Most of the time, you will discover that people enjoy helping out other people, especially if it is somebody who will really benefit from it.
- Try to be specific for the reasons you need help. People are far more understanding when they know they are helping for an important reason.

6. Seek professional help. Cognitive behavior therapy (CBT) is a psychotherapy that focuses on problem-solving and initiating behavioral change for many different types of mental disorders. Cognitive therapy is instrumental in teaching new skills that will alter thinking and behavior for a lifetime.

- CBT centers on dealing with situation thought more than on emotions.
- Therapy is open for everybody not just those with a mental disorder. In fact, at any point you would like to make a change in your life at work, home, family and friends, personal relationships or colleagues, therapy is a safe route to take.
- Cognitive therapy is also useful if you want to improve your intellect, cultural interests, learn new skills, or simply improve the overall quality of your life.

Method 3. Challenging Yourself

1. Learn a new skill. Challenge yourself to find a new skill in the office, gym, kitchen, or garage.

Pick something you are interested in and try to master it. This will help you to achieve a goal, build confidence in your abilities, and improves your mental fitness.

- Most jobs require some adaptation over time. Taking time to learn a new skill can keep you in control of your career path, boost your self-esteem, and keep your mind sharp.
- Lifelong learners are able to keep up with rapidly changing times and face the ever evolving challenges of modernity.
- Acquiring a new skill will help keep your mind operating at a high level, decrease the risk of cognitive impairment, and the overall enjoyment of better mental health.

2. Deal with stress. Stress is a part of live and is unavoidable, however, understanding what triggers your stress is important in dealing with it while keeping your mental strength intact. A balanced lifestyle is the most immediate way of handling stress, but if you find stress debilitating then you might have to go a step further and reduce stress by trying yoga or breathing exercises.

- Perform yoga as a way to help you experience your true nature – thoughts, feelings, and emotions – as a way to help you interact with the stressful environment. In short, it could factor in your quality of life.
- Taking short, three minute breaks a few times every day to stop what you are doing and inhale and exhale deeply can help clarify your thoughts, calm you down, and make you more productive. Make sure you find a quiet space so that you can concentrate on breathing as the air circulates throughout your entire body.

3. Live in the present moment. Take time everyday to try and experience all of your senses. Per-

forming these exercises will slow your body down and boost your brain power, reduce stress, and refocus your thoughts for the rest of the day. Our brains are constantly flooded with both visual and mental clutter as we endure the frenzied and chaotic world around us. Mindful exercises enable us to become more fully immersed in the present moment, and break the chain of stress and worry.

- Mindfulness is the art of experiencing the step-by-step process of ordinary, everyday activities by consciously thinking about how each sense plays a role in doing the mundane. Breathing is a key element to this exercise as you will need to concentrate on inhaling, exhaling, and tracing the path of the air as it travels throughout your body. Mindful exercises will bring the moment-by-moment awareness of thoughts, sensations, feelings, and a sense of the environment around you.
- Doing routine chores around the house can serve as mindful exercises. Whether vacuuming, ironing, or dusting, engage with each step of the process instead of performing it without thought.
- Take ten minutes every day to perform one mindful activity. Keep a journal to write down your feelings to each activity to explain in words your experience. It is important to realize the difference in performing the activity mindlessly compared to mindfully.

How to Decrease your Brain Age

With as many nerve cells as there are stars in the Milky Way (approximately 100 billion), your brain accounts for 2.5 percent of your body's total weight and uses up to 20 percent of your total energy supply. With proper use, care and knowledge, you have the means for decreasing your brain's age at any stage of your life. This topic will give you some simple tests for calculating your current brain age and will then give you some ideas for how to sharpen your mental abilities.

Part 1. Testing your Current Brain Age

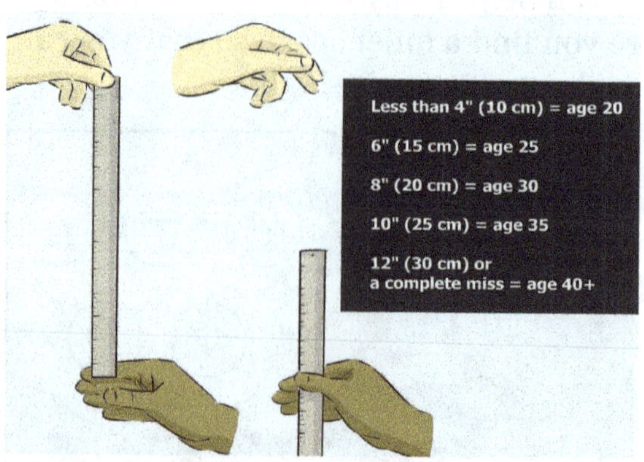

1. Check your reaction time. Ask another person to hold a 12" (30 cm) ruler in front of you.
    - Place your open hand under the ruler and have your tester drop the ruler without letting you know. Catch it when you can.

- See where you rate (distance passed when caught):
- Less than 4" (10 cm) = age 20
- 6" (15 cm) = age 25
- 8" (20 cm) = age 30
- 10" (25 cm) = age 35
- 12" (30 cm) or a complete miss = age 40+

2. Test your balance. Stand up. Raise one leg to the front with your knee bent at a right angle and hold your arms out to the sides.

- Close your eyes and see how long you can hold this position. Just make sure, especially if you're older, that you have someone there to catch you if you fall or that you have a soft place to land.
- Check your results (time passed before having to return leg to floor):
    - Over 30 seconds = age 20
    - 20 to 30 seconds = age 30
    - 15 to 20 seconds = age 40
    - 10 to 15 seconds = age 50
    - Less than 10 seconds = age 60

3. Evaluate your memory. You'll need a partner for this test.

- Write out a list of 6 different sentences. Have someone else place 2 mixed up letters (and symbols) on Line 1, 4 on Line 2, 6 on Line 3, 8 on Line 4, 10 on Line 5, and 12 on Line 6.
- Read a line and then cover that line up. Write down what you have remember next to the covered up line. Repeat this step until you've gone through each line.
- Calculate how much of each sentence you remembered correctly and write it down as a percentage. Add all 6 percentages and then divide that number by a total of 6 to get an average.
- Rate yourself (by percentage correct):
  - 100% = age 20
  - 90% = age 30
  - 80% = age 40
  - 70% = age 50
  - 60% = age 60
  - 50% = age 70
  - 40% = age 80
  - 30% or below = age 90

Part 2. Sharpening your Brain with Healthy Habits

1. Pick out foods that feed your brain. Find a balance between food types, keeping processed foods to a minimum and choosing healthy fats, proteins and carbohydrates to fuel your brain.

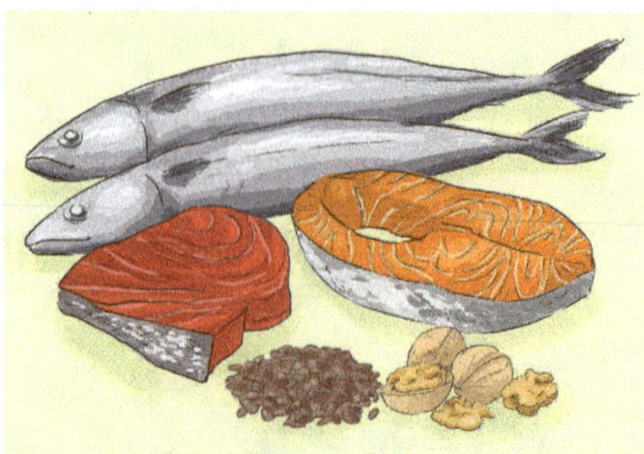

2. Choose healthy fats. Here are some things that you can do to increase your intake of good fats:

- Cook with healthy oils like olive oil.
- Add more omega 3 fats by eating foods such as salmon, walnuts and flax seeds.
- Take a PS supplement. Phosphatidylserine (PS) is a phospholipid found in abundance in your brain cells. Taking supplements of PS and other phospholipids may boost your mood, memory and concentration.

3. Try other supplements. Lecithin granules, ginkgo biloba, niacin, B12, the amino acid pyroglutamate and B5 are also helpful brain boosters.

4. Eat foods containing B vitamins and Vitamin E. Leafy greens and lean meats are good choices.

5. Eat more plant foods. When you eat a meal, half of your plate should contain either fruits or vegetables.

- Choose a variety of colorful fruits. For example, combine strawberries, plums, bananas and kiwi. You can also make a fruit salad to serve with a meal or as a meal in itself.
- Vary your colors when you eat vegetables. Mix it up by eating sweet potatoes, spinach, black beans and green peas.
- Fruits and vegetables are good sources of antioxidants. Foods that contain a lot of antioxidants and phenols help to both prevent cell damage and break down special fats that are important to your brain.

6. Drink more water Your brain consists of 85 percent water. Therefore, for the health of your brain as well as the rest of your body, drink 8 8-ounce (240 ml) of water every day.

7. Avoid foods that age your brain. These include:

- Baked goods containing white flour and processed sugar including doughnuts, cakes, cookies, pies and pastries.
- Alcohol.
- Hard cheeses and processed dairy products.
- Sugary foods like soft drinks, fruit drinks and sugary breakfast cereals.
- Creamy sauces.

- Hydrogenated oils and trans fats.
- Mayonnaise.
- Packaged convenience foods and fast food.

8. Exercise your body. After age 25, our taken-for-granted physical health begins to decline, helped along by inactive lifestyles. Physical exercise is important for your brain because it provides much needed oxygen; improved blood flow to the brain helps the growth of new brain cell "branches" (dendrites).

- People who exercise have been shown to have denser brains than those who do not. Loss of brain density and volume becomes more prevalent as we age and is a major factor in mental decline.
- Weight bearing exercise has been shown to improve levels of serotonin and dopamine in adults, which are two brain chemicals related directly to brain aging.

9. Practice good sleeping habits. Sleep is a powerful way to combat aging.

- Research has shown that a regular 8-hour sleep pattern slows age decline and protects people against chronic age-related memory loss.
- Go to bed at the same time every night and rise at the same time every morning. Make sure to get 7 to 8 hours of sleep. Your brain will be grateful — and younger — for the much needed consistent and regular recharging.

Part 3. Sharpen your Brain with Mental Exercises

1. Solve puzzles. Puzzles such as crosswords, Sudoku, trivia games, brainteasers, mazes and word puzzles are all superb mental workouts.

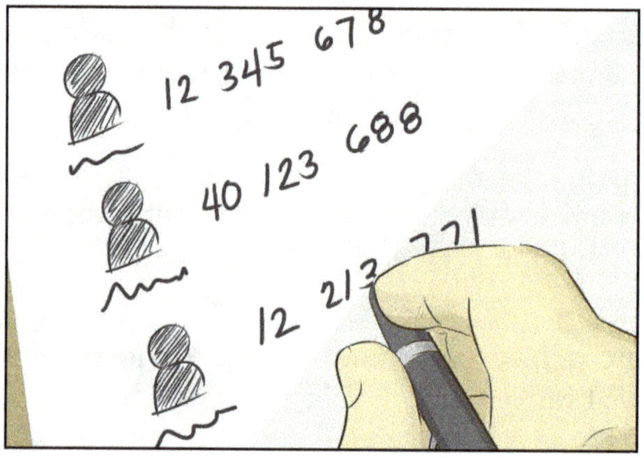

2. Memorize sequences of numbers, letters, words or symbols. Do this with a friend so that you can both improve your memory.

3. Play memory games. For example, place different objects on a tray, try to memorize them and then cover them up and repeat what they are. Continuously increase the number of objects you're trying to remember.

4. Play games on your computer. The best games require you to solve mathematical problems quickly. Puzzles that require you to race against the clock are also helpful.

5. Take advantage of down time. Try to remember chunks of text, phone numbers, lines of printed letters or anything else that you can spot around you.

- Try to remember things about people sitting near you. Close your eyes and try to remember things about them and check if you got it right (take care not to stare).
- You can also do this with pictures in a magazine that are filled with action or elements. Stare at a picture for 10 seconds. Then, write down as many things as possible that you can remember about it and compare your recall after.
- Become a good storyteller. This is a great way to keep your memories alive and helps you to perceive past events in a positive light, by using the storyteller's technique of finding a moral, a lesson, or a confirmation within the past experience.

6. Read lots of good books. Reading has long been a guaranteed way to keep your brain alert and attuned to new ideas and perspectives.

7. Try something new. "Neuroplasticity" is the term used to explain the brain's ability to reorganize its neural pathways based on a new experiences.

- Try a new way of doing something that you've always done. This is a really good way to create new patterns in your brain.
- Learn a new skill. Learning new skills will continuously push your brain and will give you opportunities to meet new people, sample new experiences and introduce variety into your life. Trying something new can actually help you to "declutter" your brain and remove irrelevant information and replace it with useful information.

8. Learn a new language. Teaching yourself a new language is one of the most rewarding mental workouts. When you're proficient, you can plan a trip to a country that speaks that language to give yourself a rewarding new experience.

9. Try tutoring. When you teach others, you draw on past experiences and apply them in a different way. You will also draw on many problem-solving skills when teaching or tutoring.

Part 4. Decrease your Brain's Age with Good Mental Health Practices

1. Cope with stress. Stress is good for you in small doses because it keeps you on your toes and it helps to remind you that you're alive and need to be careful in certain situations. Excess, pronounced, and never-ending stress typical of our modern way of living, however, kills brains cells and ages your brain faster. To decrease your brain age, reduce your exposure to and intolerance of stress by finding ways that minimize it, ways that work for you. Some ideas include:

- Meditating. Meditation is one of the more effective methods for reducing stress in your life and it can be done at home, at work and even while traveling.
- Taking up a physical activity that releases stress, such as yoga, martial arts, kickboxing or tennis.
- Learning to be more assertive and to express yourself. Assertive people are better able to state their needs and wants politely but firmly. Expressing yourself clearly and refusing to allow yourself to be used or swayed by others is a good way of keeping stress at bay.
- Exercising more. Exercise wards off the effects of stress by burning off the stress hormones and chasing away the cortisol that destroys brain cells. Mood improves with exercise too, as noradrenaline is secreted and endorphins enter the bloodstream. These substances give you a lift and help to ward off depression.

2. Improve your attitude. Your attitude affects brain activity and influences your mood and emotional state. A positive outlook that allows you to maintain a belief in your value and self-worth will allow you to live a fulfilled life in which your brain remains open to new possibilities. On the other hand, constant negative thinking can easily shut you off from continued learning and growth, which will cause your brain to age faster.

- Learn to control negative thinking. The first step is to recognize negative thoughts. The second step is to change the thoughts to something more realistic and positive. Changing negative thinking is the same as changing any other bad habit. The more you practice positive thinking, the more your brain will respond.
- Work on your emotional intelligence. When you have emotional intelligence, you can recognize your emotions, reason with them and use them to enhance thought. You will be more creative, make better decisions and implement positive solutions to problems. The better you get at mastering your own emotions, the better you'll become at enabling constructive emotions in others as well, which will create more fruitful connections in your life.
- Reframe the Past in your mind. While you cannot change the past, you can change your attitude toward it and avoid slipping into a victim mentality. Re-examine events that brought you shame, guilt, humiliation, sadness and fear so that you can let them go and move forward. You'll decrease your brain age with a better attitude because you'll remove useless, energy-sapping thoughts and replace them with healthier, forward-looking and self-forgiving thoughts that will energize you.

3. Do What You Love. People who love what they're doing in life tend to experience a greater sense of purpose and happiness. You may not be in your dream job, activity or relationship, but you can find things to be grateful for in the life you're leading. Mix up work tasks every day and pursue plenty of other activities to add playfulness, interest and fun into your life.

4. Give mental exercises 100 percent of your effort. When undertaking mental workouts, be sure to focus and concentrate properly. You won't get benefits from simply going through the motions – you must really throw yourself into doing the mental workout activities with full attention.

Part 5. Other Tips for Decreasing your Brain's Age

1. Nurture your spiritual self. Whatever your beliefs or lack of them, nurturing your spiritual self or connecting to the awe and wonder of life is an important aspect of keeping your brain young.

- Our brains are wired for spiritual experiences, such as times that we take a holistic approach to our place in the world and seek complete well-being and a sense of purpose.
- Practice prayer, meditation, reflection, taking time out or whatever allows you to focus on your spiritual self. This will give your brain the space to make connections and to seek "the flow" of life in which heart, mind, and body all work as one.
- Nurturing your spiritual self increases your compassion for both yourself and for others, allowing you to connect better with others and thereby enhance your brain functioning.

2. Choose purple to boost your brain. Purple, including shades of violet and lavender, may improve your ability to think and achieve. Purple is associated with memory, imagination, creativity, wisdom, and strategic problem-solving, so adding more of this color into your life can help focus your brain.

- Buy some purple supplies. Buy purple picture frames, office supplies or even a purple cell phone.
- Surround yourself with purple. Paint your walls purple. Wear purple clothes or accessories and put purple furniture in your thinking zones in your home.
- Construct a purple visualization board to help you prioritize the most important things in your life.

- Hang a map of the world inside a purple frame. Stick purple stick-pins into the places around the world that you'd like to visit or revisit.

3. Be a social butterfly and build social support networks. A lonely brain tends to age faster and while you don't need to be the life and soul of the party, you do need the lift that regular connection with other people can provide you.

- Don't just hang people of your own age group, especially if you're older. People tend to think similarly to those they spend time with and "feeling old" is catching
- Older people tend to prefer to be around people they're most familiar with while younger people tend to enjoy meeting new people and getting to know a wider variety of people. If you're going to keep your brain younger, think young by mixing up your social contacts and spending time with people in all age groups.

4. Go back in time. Thinking about your youth, and of memories you had when you were young, can keep your brain young.

- In 1979, a Harvard psychology professor Ellen Langer created an experiment in which elderly people were sent to live in a house set up as if it were 1959, 20 years earlier. They had to watch 1950s TV, wear clothing from the era and act as if they were living in the '50s. Those who participated in the study displayed improved recall, intelligence and even eyesight. They even appeared younger when before and after photos of them were compared.

- A study by John Bargh showed that people who thought about words related to aging slowed down after they did the test. Aim to think mostly of words relating to youth, vitality, energy, and pep whenever you consider your own age.
- Seek to see yourself as younger than your biological age. How you think about your age is as important as what you eat and how much you exercise. Much aging is in the mind. If you live and think like a younger person and your brain will definitely cooperate.

5. Avoid multi-tasking. Multi-tasking reduces your brain's effectiveness and can cause you stress. Instead, complete single tasks with greater focus.

6. Reduce the time you spend watching TV. Instead, choose pastimes that are more interactive and require brain input. Only use TV viewing as an occasional treat.

How to Keep your Brain in Top Shape

Keeping your brain in top shape is a great way to improve your quality of life. Start by eating nutritious foods, working out often, and getting enough sleep. To challenge your brain, try out puzzling, gaming, or learning a new instrument or language. Maintaining a positive mindset is important as well. With a little bit of work, your brain can be running on all cylinders.

Method 1. Challenging Your Mind

1. Go outside your comfort zone. Your brain is like a muscle and requires challenges and novelty in order to more fully develop. Once you determine that a certain area of study or mental activity is outside your comfort zone, push yourself to attempt it anyway. A good rule is that comfort is not good for your brain. Aim for unsteadiness and uncertainty in learning.

- For example, if math is difficult for you, then you might want to spend some more time working on it. This may be better for your brain than moving on to a more comfortable subject.
- Try something new now and then. For example, if you are not naturally athletic, try doing something that requires athletic skills, such as playing a game of softball with friends or taking an exercise class.

2. Select challenging reading. Instead of just starting a new book that catches your eye, think about what subjects interest you and seek out books in those areas. Begin your reading at the ground level and work your way up to master works. This is one way to achieve a degree of mastery in a subject. You'll also find that your vocabulary and ability to explain difficult concepts will improve as well.

- For example, if you are curious about physics you might want to start with a documentary and then move on to more specialized books by famous physicists.

3. Learn a new language. Enroll in a local college course. Work with a tutor on a weekly basis. Or, purchase online language software and teach yourself. When you work on a new language it activates parts of your brain that remain generally dormant otherwise. Once you get comfortable with one language, move on to the next and so on.

4. Learn to play a musical instrument. Take a lesson with a private tutor. Enroll in a local college course. Or, find an online or digital instructor who offers introductory to advanced lessons. Mastering an instrument can also give you a confidence boost.

- Even listening to music can have a positive effect on your brain. Your IQ may experience a temporary boost after listening to songs by Mozart or other artists and composers.

5. Play video games, but cut out TV. Get out a game console and play at least 15 minutes each day. Working your way through video games can actually increase the number of cells in the left side of your brain. It can also improve your reaction time and hand-to-eye coordination.

- In contrast, watching television may overload your brain with useless information, which can cause mental slowdowns. Long hours of TV watching has been linked to ADHD, too.
- Keep in mind that you can overdo it with video games as well. Try to moderate your video game activity, and if you feel like you are playing too much, then cut back.
- Video games, such as Minecraft, can help people to develop social connections that extend outside of the gaming sphere. Instead of becoming the antisocial stereotype, part-time gamers can develop prosocial attitudes.

6. Play chess or solve puzzles. Buy a chess set and challenge friends and family to a game. Go online and join a chess club. Look up the crossword or Sudoku puzzle in your local newspaper. Or, find an online puzzle site and subscribe to regular emails. Puzzling and strategy games teach your brain to remain calm under pressure and to come up with creative solutions to problems.

Method 2. Getting in the Proper Mindset

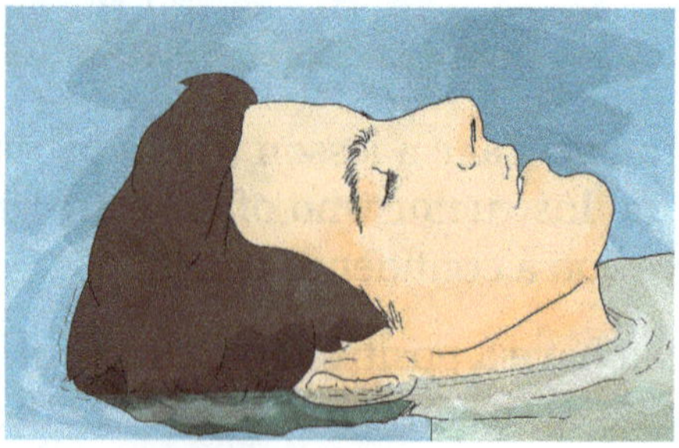

1. Lower your stress levels. Take a yoga class, plan a relaxing date night each week, or create relaxing routines, such as taking a bubble bath after work. Chronic stress can push you toward dementia and other brain disorders, so relaxing can go a long way towards improving cognitive performance.

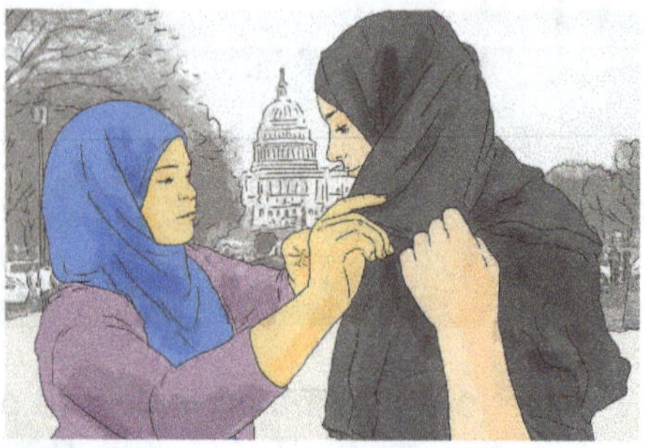

2. Create social connections to maintain a positive outlook. Invite coworkers out for social activities.

Participate in social clubs to meet new people. Try to talk with people whenever you go out instead of staying focused on your phone. Every time we make positive human contact our brains experience an uptick in good chemicals, such as endorphins. Be social and your brain will thank you.

3. Meditate and practice reflection. Take a formal meditation class at a yoga studio or recreation center near you. Spend at least 15 minutes each day meditating or reflecting. You can even sit in bed at night, clear your mind, and think about the day's events. This gives your brain a jumpstart on its work once you go to sleep.

- To enter a meditative state, you might need to repeat a word or phrase, such as, "relax," or "reflect." Try to mediate in an area where you will be undisturbed and can try to slide into a semi-conscious frame of mind.
- You can, of course, meditate for longer than 15 minutes if you like.

4. Establish routines for simple tasks. For things that you do every day, try to establish a pattern of how to behave or what to do and stick with it. For example, when you come home at night, place your keys at the same spot in your house. Taking away any decision-making in simple scenarios like this frees up your brainpower to tackle more complex problems.

- For example, it is good idea to write down all of your appointments in a calendar or planner so that you don't have to worry or stress about remembering the basic details.
- Making a habit of tidying up and putting things away after you use them will create a clean, orderly environment for living and working.

Method 3. Maintaining Good Health

1. Consult with your doctor. It's a good idea to see your general doctor before you decide to boost your brain power. They will likely run a series of blood tests to make sure that no physical ailments will halt your progress. Some conditions, such as high blood pressure or diabetes, can negatively impact your brain's ability to process and store information.

2. Get at least 8 hours of sleep per night. Going to sleep early and waking early as well is one way to improve your brain power. So, set a consistent bedtime and rising time and try to stick with them. 8 hours of uninterrupted sleep is just enough for your brain to process information and to prepare fully for the next day.

- To minimize sleep interruptions, turn off your phone and let anyone you live with know your nighttime schedule. Every moment of sleep disruption raises your brain's stress levels.

3. Eat a balanced diet. Your brain will run best with unprocessed foods, lean meats, lots of fresh

produce, and healthy fats. Eating healthy can improve both your brain's memory capacity and overall functioning. Sugar, on the other hand, can slow down brain cell connections and lead to a general feeling of mental fogginess.

- It is especially important to add foods rich in omega-3 fatty acids, such as broiled or baked fish, to your diet. These can boost the spaces in your brain set aside for memory.

4. Exercise at least 3 times a week. Create a workout regimen that includes both cardio and weight resistance motions. This routine should take a minimum of 30 minutes. If you want to work out more than 3 times, then you will likely see even more cognitive benefits. Exercise increases blood flow to your brain and keep its cells active and refreshed.

5. Maintain an upright posture. Keep your spine straight, shoulder back, arms uncrossed, and stomach sucked in towards your spine. Check each hour to see that you are maintaining these positions. Poor posture sends a negative message to your brain that can contribute to depression and slowed down memory. Holding yourself in a positive way can push your brain in that direction too.

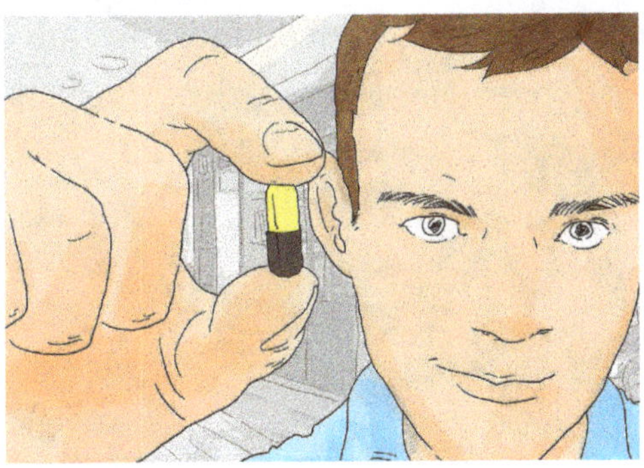

6. Take supplements. Talk with your doctor about your diet to see if a multivitamin or supplement

might be a good fit for you. Fish oil supplements, in particular, are often linked with improved memory and overall brain functioning. Your doctor can also order a blood test to see if your levels are too low on any other important nutrients, such as vitamins B, C, D, and E.

- Human growth hormone (HGH) supplements can be useful for certain people older than 30 who are trying to combat memory loss and brain slowdown.

How to Keep Mentally Fit

Read these steps to learn how to keep mentally fit. They'll surely help.

Steps

1. Keep your brain active. Read the papers, solve crosswords, figure out puzzles, socialize, and keep contact with people.

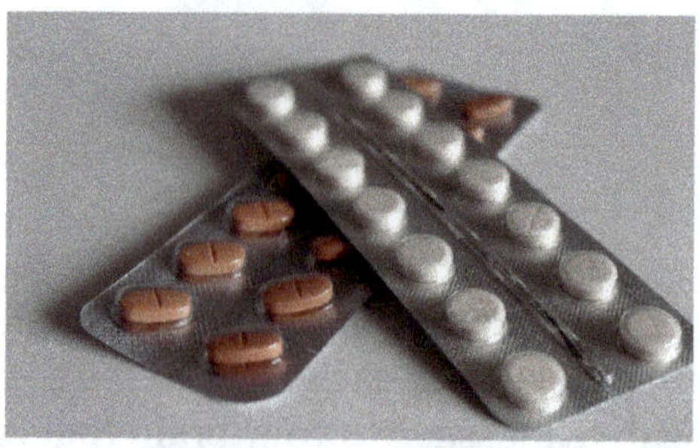

2. Discuss the kinds of medication you are using with your family doctor. Some medicines (including sleeping pills) and certain combinations of medicines may adversely affect your memory.

3. Eat healthy. Lack of variety in your food may lead to vitamin deficiency, which can lead to

memory problems. Some researchers say that the use of turmeric reduces the risk of AD. Others think a diet high in fruits, vegetables, cereals, but low in meat and dairy products helps.

4. Drink in moderation. The older you get, the less your brain can cope with alcohol.

5. Take plenty of exercise. Improved blood circulation reduces the risk of disorders such as vascular dementia.

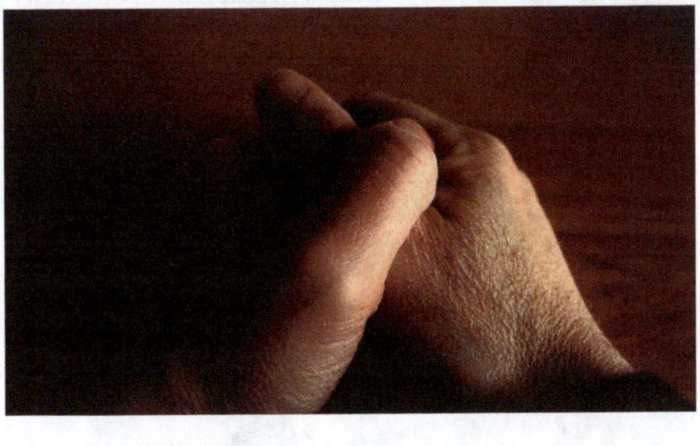

6. See your doctor if you feel that you- or one of your loved ones- isn't behaving or thinking normally.

How to Nourish your Mental Health Daily

Having good mental health positively benefits your life in a multitude of ways. When your overall psychological well-being is in good shape, you are better able to cope with life's ups and downs. Nourishing your mental health on a daily basis fosters stronger resilience to stress, supports physical health, improves your mood and outlook, and increases your life satisfaction. Learn how to boost mental health everyday by maximizing your social connections, nurturing your body, and finding meaning and purpose in life.

Method 1. Connecting with others Often

1. Hang out with friends and family every day. Having a strong and supportive network of friends and family is key to optimal mental health. Social interaction helps boost resilience to stressful events and even helps you live longer. When you spend time with others who make you feel good, your body generates hormones that lift the mood and fight stress.

- At the beginning of each week, try to schedule in contact with close friends and family on a daily basis. Your contact can be a simple phone call or a lunch date. Schedule in these connections just as you would a doctor's appointment or a career function. While it's nice to forge friendships online through social media and group forums, aim to meet some friends in- person regularly. This allows you to take a break from your daily grind and satisfies your innate need for social connections.

2. Have dinner with family each night. Mealtime with the family is often overlooked. However, sharing meals with the people you love has a host of advantages—not least of which is the chance

connect with one another. Imagine the traditional family meal: each member has the chance to share big and little details about daily life that might otherwise get buried in the hustle and bustle of the day. Everyone has a special opportunity to give and receive attention.

- Research shows that the tradition of the family meal is declining, unfortunately. Only about 30 to 35% of families enjoy at least 3 meals weekly together. It's understandable that everyone is busy, but make a goal to all sit down and share a meal together a few times a week. Everyone will benefit when you do.
- If you don't live with your family or they live far away, try to have a friend or roommate join you for dinner as often as possible. You can reap the same benefits by dining with your best bud.

3. Play with your pet each day after school or work. When you think of connection, that of the animal variety may not immediately come to mind, but it should. If you have ever owned a dog, cat or other pet, you probably know all too well the level of joy and fulfillment animals can offer. Owning pets provides a range of benefits that contribute to positive mental and physical health, such as:

- Reducing depression
- Lowering blood pressure
- Boosting relaxation
- Producing a stimulus for exercise
- Helping you meet other pet-owners

4. Volunteer a few days a week. Helping out in your local community offers a wide range of

opportunities to meet new people and connect with others. This not only satisfies your natural human desire for social interaction, but it also affords you a sense of purpose and meaning. Dedicating a few hours each day or week to a good cause can help you to feel like you are making an impact, resulting in stronger self-confidence and greater well-being.

- Look for ways you can contribute in your community. Animal shelters, nursing homes, homeless shelters, religious organizations, and schools typically have a need for volunteers. Contact these groups and see how you can go yourself some good by doing for others.

Method 2. Caring for your Body Every Day

1. Consume a healthy diet every day. Eating foods filled with empty calories, excess fat, salt, and sugar will only slow down your cognitive abilities and leave you feeling tired and drained. Selecting nutritious foods from all food groups delivers essential vitamins and nutrients to your body for abundant energy, clear thinking, and a positive mindset.

- Enjoy a diet rich in fruits, vegetables, whole grains, lean sources of protein, low-fat dairy and plenty of water. Eat several small meals per day and include healthy snacks such as nuts, seeds, dried fruits, and raw vegetables. Avoid junk food, fast food, and foods that are overly processed (e.g. have long, extensive ingredient lists).

2. Exercise on a daily basis. Staying physically active is a terrific way to foster good mental health. Exercise not only supports physical fitness, it also lifts your mood and gives you energy to function

effectively. Engaging in heart-pumping exercise produces feel-good chemicals in the body called endorphins. These chemicals give you the characteristic "high" that you feel after exercising.

- Most studies suggest that you should get in at least 30 minutes of physical activity on most days of the week. What you do, however, is up to you. Pick and choose between activities that you like and that challenge you physically. You can run, swim, weight train, dance, or kick box—just get moving to reap the benefits.
- Aim to get a workout in each morning before you do anything else. Doing so gives you a burst of energy to move through your day and prevents you from skipping it later.

3. Make sleep a priority each night. Rest is important for long-lasting mental health, too. You may think that sacrificing a few hours' sleep will give you the advantage to get ahead in life, but doing this regularly can actually detract from your overall well-being. Feeling sluggish or tired while at work or school can cause you to make mistakes and perform poorly.

- Aim for 7 to 9 hours of sleep per night. Doing so can increase productivity during the day, help you stay alert, boost your immune system to prevent illness, and fight off mental health issues like depression or anxiety.
- To optimize your sleep quality implement a few strategies. These may include creating an unwinding routine each night with activities such as journaling, reading, taking a hot bath and making a cup of tea. Try to rise and retire at the same times each day. Turn off your tech devices at least 30 minutes before bed. And, make your sleep environment comfortable by lowering the temperature of the room, removing distractions, and using black-out curtains.

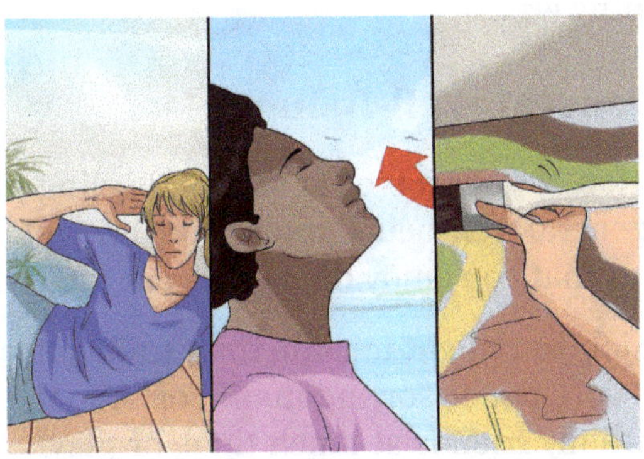

4. Incorporate stress-management into your daily schedule. If you feel stressed out on a day-to-

day basis, your mental health (and physical health) may suffer. Although it's impossible to completely avoid stress, it's a good idea to have strategies in place to prevent stress from affecting your life satisfaction. Develop a toolbox of useful skills that help you keep stress at bay.

- Your stress relief toolbox may include relaxation techniques, such as deep breathing, meditation, or visualization. In addition, incorporate activities/hobbies that bring you joy, such as listening to music, painting, writing, or getting a massage.
- Don't forget that eating an unhealthy diet, skipping your work out, and failing to sleep can all worsen the effects of stress. Good mental health requires consistently attending to your physical and emotional needs on a regular basis.
- You can also develop a spiritual practice as a way to relax. This may include meditation, prayer, or some other spiritual practice that you find satisfying.

5. Avoid alcohol and drugs. During tough times, substances like alcohol and drugs can seem like a good idea. These substances often help people numb their feelings or provide a temporary mood lift. However, in the long run, alcohol and drugs only worsen the core problem. Minimize your use of alcohol and say "no" to drugs for overall health and wellness.

- If you have trouble quitting alcohol or drugs, it's important to get help as soon as possible. Excessive use of either can lead to problems functioning at work or school and issues in your relationships. See a professional counselor or therapist to help you overcome alcohol or drug abuse in a healthy way.

Method 3. Promoting General Well-Being

1. Identify sources of satisfaction at your job or at school. Feeling fulfilled at work or in school is a great way to promote your general well-being and to nourish your mental health. To do this, try making a list of all of the things that you enjoy doing for your job or for school.

- For example, for your job you might include things like interacting with customers, working closely with my coworkers, or sorting mail. For school, you might include things like, math class, visiting with my friends at lunch time, or playing soccer in physical education class.

- If you are working a job that you do not find satisfying or that makes you feel unhappy, then it might be time for a change. Start looking into other jobs that you might like to do. If you are struggling to find things that make you happy at school, then you might consider talking with a school counselor to get some help with identifying ways that you can improve your school experience.

2. Find ways to stimulate your mind. Mental stimulation is an important part of your overall well-being. You may feel intellectually stimulated while you are working or in certain classes, or you may need to create your own opportunities for intellectual stimulation.

- For example, you could try reading a new book, doing a daily crossword puzzle, or playing intellectually stimulating games with your family, such as chess or Scrabble.

3. Learn how to process and express your emotions. Finding healthy ways to process and express your emotions is important for nourishing your mental health and it may also help you to feel better overall. Try to develop a strategy for processing and expressing your emotions, such as writing about them in a journal or calling a friend and telling them what is going on.

- If you had a rough day, then you might take 15 minutes to notice how you are feeling, label the feeling, and then to write about the source of this feeling. For example, you might notice that you feel angry and attribute it to getting a low grade on your math test. You might write about how you feel angry at yourself because you did not study for the test.
- Make sure that you identify a healthy way to deal with the emotion, such as going for a run, playing some music, or engaging in a favorite hobby, such as cooking or knitting.

4. Leverage your personal strengths. A powerful way to boost mental health is by engaging in meaningful work. You may have heard the phrase "do what you love, love what you do." There's no better prescription for a healthy, fulfilling life. However, doing what you love doesn't necessarily have to refer to a job or career. Loving your job can be an exhilarating part of life, but there are also many other ways to contribute in a meaningful way.

- The secret to doing meaningful work is using your personal strengths. First, you must identify your strengths by either reviewing the areas/skillset you're good at, asking for feedback from others, and completing a strengths-based questionnaire, such as the VIA Character Strengths Questionnaire.

- Once you have figured out what your strengths are, you can leverage them in your everyday life. For example, if a major character strength of yours is integrity, you could use this strength to your advantage. Take on the role of treasurer in a community organization or become an ambassador for a global fundraiser since a person of integrity is a great choice for handling money.
- Find as many ways as you can each day to put your personal strengths to work. As you do this, you will notice yourself becoming more empowered and satisfied with your life.

5. Set realistic goals and do one thing to reach them daily. Everyone has aspirations for the future. You may want to become a doctor, travel the world, or go back to college. However small or big your dreams are, you can only reach them by completing manageable chunks at a time. Adopting the habit of setting realistic and attainable goals allows you to notice and feel accomplished about your achievements, and, therefore, increase your quality of life.

- One method for setting realistic goals is to use the S.M.A.R.T. acronym. S.M.A.R.T. goals are those that are:
    - Specific- be clear about what you want to do.
    - Measurable- be clear about how you can keep track of progress.
    - Attainable- be sure that the goal actually is achievable through action.
    - Relevant- be sure that the goal is relevant to you and your dreams.
    - Time-bound- be sure to set a firm deadline that is challenging, but reasonable.

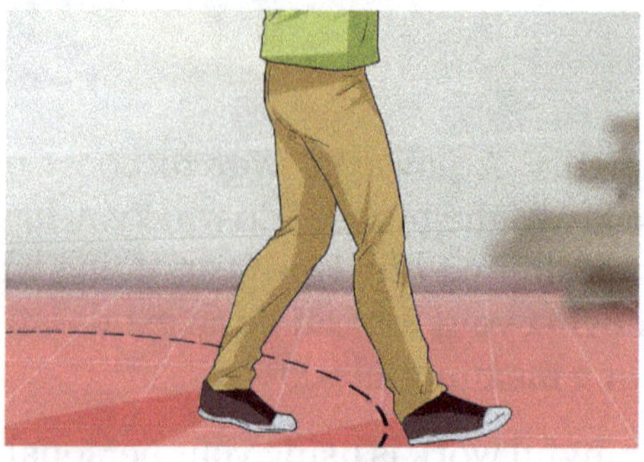

6. Step out of your comfort zone often. The best way to maximize your satisfaction of life and nourish mental health is by showing steady growth. How do you do that? You grow by challenging yourself and getting out of your comfort zone.

- If you always did what was safe and familiar you would be closed off from other areas of potential that you can develop. Being challenged beyond your comfort zones creates a bit of good stress so that you are pushed to learn, invent, create, and transform.
- Take strides to challenge yourself daily by putting fear aside and asking yourself "what would I do today if I could not fail?" Whatever pops into your head, go for it.
- Plus, you shouldn't be afraid of making mistakes because they are simply growing and learning opportunities. Reframe how you look at failure by giving it new meaning—think of FAIL as a "first attempt in learning."

7. Spend 20 minutes in nature each day. If you are searching for a small way to boost your mental wellness each day, look no further than beyond your front door. Getting outside into the natural world delivers unbelievable advantages to physical, mental, emotional, and spiritual health. Many people feel more connected with to a higher power or the universe when they step outside. Not to mention, getting a bit of sunlight and fresh air can be incredibly refreshing.

- Studies reveal that spending time outdoors can reduce depression, increase energy, and improve one's overall well-being. People who spent just 20 minutes in nature felt revitalized and had a greater resistance to illness.
- Take a book outdoors and read. Put your dog on a leash and walk through the woods. Or, simply take a few minutes each day to enjoy through your garden. Any time spent outside is an investment to your mental health.

Permissions

All chapters in this book are published with permission under the Creative Commons Attribution Share Alike License or equivalent. Every chapter published in this book has been scrutinized by our experts. Their significance has been extensively debated. The topics covered herein carry significant information for a comprehensive understanding. They may even be implemented as practical applications or may be referred to as a beginning point for further studies.

We would like to thank the editorial team for lending their expertise to make the book truly unique. They have played a crucial role in the development of this book. Without their invaluable contributions this book wouldn't have been possible. They have made vital efforts to compile up to date information on the varied aspects of this subject to make this book a valuable addition to the collection of many professionals and students.

This book was conceptualized with the vision of imparting up-to-date and integrated information in this field. To ensure the same, a matchless editorial board was set up. Every individual on the board went through rigorous rounds of assessment to prove their worth. After which they invested a large part of their time researching and compiling the most relevant data for our readers.

The editorial board has been involved in producing this book since its inception. They have spent rigorous hours researching and exploring the diverse topics which have resulted in the successful publishing of this book. They have passed on their knowledge of decades through this book. To expedite this challenging task, the publisher supported the team at every step. A small team of assistant editors was also appointed to further simplify the editing procedure and attain best results for the readers.

Apart from the editorial board, the designing team has also invested a significant amount of their time in understanding the subject and creating the most relevant covers. They scrutinized every image to scout for the most suitable representation of the subject and create an appropriate cover for the book.

The publishing team has been an ardent support to the editorial, designing and production team. Their endless efforts to recruit the best for this project, has resulted in the accomplishment of this book. They are a veteran in the field of academics and their pool of knowledge is as vast as their experience in printing. Their expertise and guidance has proved useful at every step. Their uncompromising quality standards have made this book an exceptional effort. Their encouragement from time to time has been an inspiration for everyone.

The publisher and the editorial board hope that this book will prove to be a valuable piece of knowledge for students, practitioners and scholars across the globe.

Index

Printed in the USA
CPSIA information can be obtained
at www.ICGtesting.com
LVHW080031211023
761596LV00010BA/1712